First Christmas Projects for Woodcarvers

Larry Green &
Mike Altman

With photography
by Steve Smith

Schiffer Publishing Ltd
4880 Lower Valley Road, Atglen, PA 19310 USA

DEDICATION

From Larry and Mike: To Douglas Congdon-Martin, Senior Editor at Schiffer Publishing, for his wisdom, assistance, creativity, and patience. His helpful, cheerful spirit has been a great encouragement to us. He is a good friend!

Library of Congress Catalog Card Number: 97-68641

Designed by Laurie A. Smucker

ISBN: 0-7643-0369-4
Printed in China

Published by Schiffer Publishing Ltd.
4880 Lower Valley Road
Atglen, PA 19310
Phone: (610) 593-1777; Fax: (610) 593-2002
E-mail: schifferbk@aol.com
Please write for a free catalog.
This book may be purchased from the publisher.
Please include $3.95 for shipping.
Try your bookstore first.

We are interested in hearing from authors with book ideas on related subjects.

CONTENTS

ACKNOWLEDGMENTS

Thanks to Tom Brown and Mac Profitt for your insights.

Thanks to Shari Conley and Tracy Naylor for your help.

Thanks to John Krantz who keeps me supplied with great carving wood.

THE *FIRST PROJECTS* FOLKS

Larry Green lives in Knoxville, Tennessee where he serves as Director of Admissions for Johnson Bible College. He is the author of *Carving Boots and Shoes, Caricature Relief Carving, Carving the Old Woman's Shoe, Carving Comic Clocks, and First Projects for Woodcarvers*. He has been carving for over twenty years and is a member of the Southern Highland Craft Guild. Larry has taught carving at the John C. Campbell Folk School in Brasstown, North Carolina. Larry has produced a sixty minute video called *Carving a Cowboy Boot with Larry Green*.

Mike Altman is a guy who likes to draw and be recognized. If you see him, wave and say hello. Mike has co-authored five books with Larry.

Steve Smith lives in Knoxville, Tennessee where he serves as a Professor at Johnson Bible College. Steve specializes in aquatic carvings with an emphasis on miniatures. He photographed the last five of Larry and Mike's books.

INTRODUCTION

The FIRST PROJECTS series of books has been in the making since the first day I picked up a knife and started woodcarving. If it had not been for a wood carver who was willing to teach me, I believe my attempts at carving would have ended in frustration. Since I do not have that natural talent, an artist's eye, I have had to really work at carving. Some of my friends tell me I have a lot more work to do. The men and women who have encouraged and given me advice saved me wasted time and mistakes. The goals for FIRST PROJECTS are to inform, instruct, encourage, and challenge.

Mike and I have designed FIRST CHRISTMAS PROJECTS for the new woodcarver. You notice we did not include such words as "complete guide," "everything you wanted to know," or "a complete course" in the title. This is not a complete work on wood carving, but rather a starting place.

The general focus of the book is to introduce you to woodcarving safety, knives, palm carving tools, helpful items and "in the round" carving. "In the round carving" encompasses figures that are 3-dimensional: humans, birds, aquatic, animals. I encourage you to investigate chip carving and relief carving. There are many fine books available on these types of carving. When I started carving, full color, step by step books were rare. Now you can probably find a book on just about any subject you wish to carve.

The step by step cuts I make in the book are based on many years of carving experience. Each picture illustrates where the wood is to be removed and does not necessarily show the only way.

THE PROJECTS

I think it is good idea to carve the stocking first. Why? There is less detail. Then move to the snowman and then to the Santa.

I suggest you carve each project several times before moving on to the next. I do this all the time. In getting ready for the book, I know I carved at least twenty of the Sleeping Santas. (some of my carving friends said I probably should have carved more.) This process helps you compare your work with past efforts and see improvement. In wood carving, improvement sometimes comes in small doses. Don't be discouraged. Keep at it. Our projects can acquaint you with your tools, grain direction, and proportions.

Some of my fondest memories of Christmas come from the stockings that were hung on our fake fireplace. They held many wonderful surprises. Our stocking pattern design lends itself to all kinds of creative painting and thoughtful ways of finishing. Our snowman will help you understand grain direction, rounding and proportions. In carving a human face, new carvers seem to have the most difficulty with eyes. We designed our Santa with his hat over the eyes, therefore no eyes to worry about. Schiffer Publishing has many excellent books that feature complete Santas. We do hope you enjoy the projects!

The three projects (Christmas Stocking Ornament, Snowman, and Sleeping Santa Ornament) were created and selected because of their design. We have not used the words "simple," "quick," or "easy" to describe the three projects. These terms are relative to the individual who attempts to carve the projects. We don't want to confuse anyone by saying they are "simple" or "easy" projects. However, we do feel they are suited for beginners with limited carving experience.

A GREAT RESOURCE FOR THE NEW CARVER

One important resource for the wood carver is The National Wood Carvers Association, 7424 Miami Avenue, Cincinnati, Ohio 45243. In 1997 they had a membership of over 50,000. The membership is growing every day. I encourage you to contact the NWCA for membership information.

The Association publishes a bimonthly magazine called *Chip Chats.* It contains articles on carving, tool sharpening, press releases on new books, reports on carving shows. Each issue contains a calendar of wood carving events across the nation. The March-April issue contains the Annual Sources of Supply Listing of books, tools & supplies, workbenches, woodburners, patterns, blanks, rough-outs, kits, and videotapes.

When you write the NWCA for information, include a self-addressed, stamped envelope. NWCA is a non-profit corporation.

SAFETY

Safety is an important consideration in wood carving. You will do your body some damage when the knife or gouge slips and finds its way into your hand or leg. You will be using sharp knives and carving tools so the potential for injury is always present. No one is exempt from being cut. We have included safety tips we encourage you to consider.

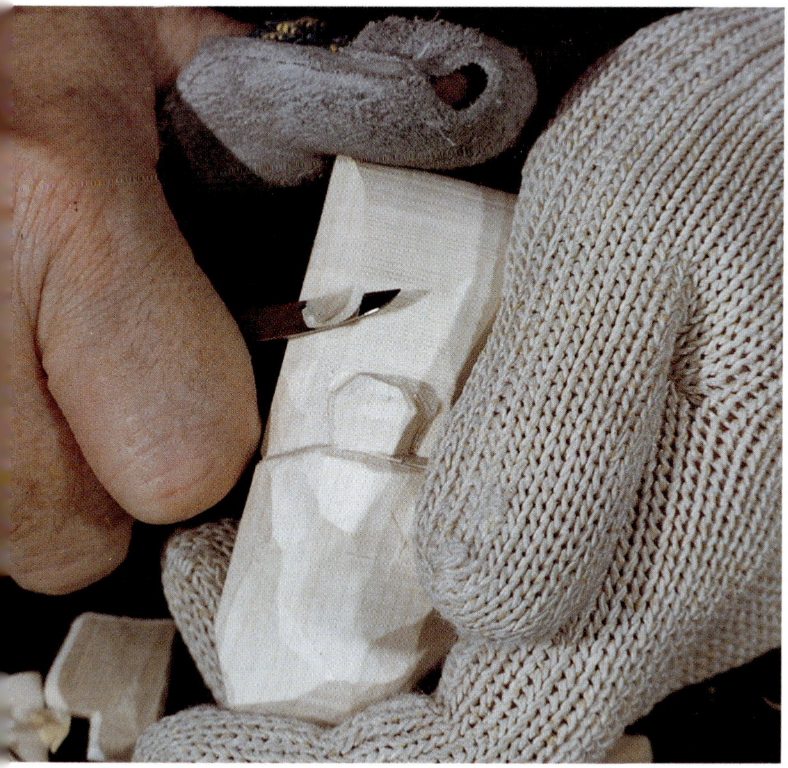

SAFETY TIP # 1: **Think before you make a cut!** If this tools slips, where is it going to go? Will it go into your hand or leg? You should never cut toward exposed skin. It is easy to get so focused on removing the wood to create a work of art that you forget the danger involved with the knife or gouge. Also, don't hurry! Wood carving is an art form to be enjoyed, not a race against the clock.

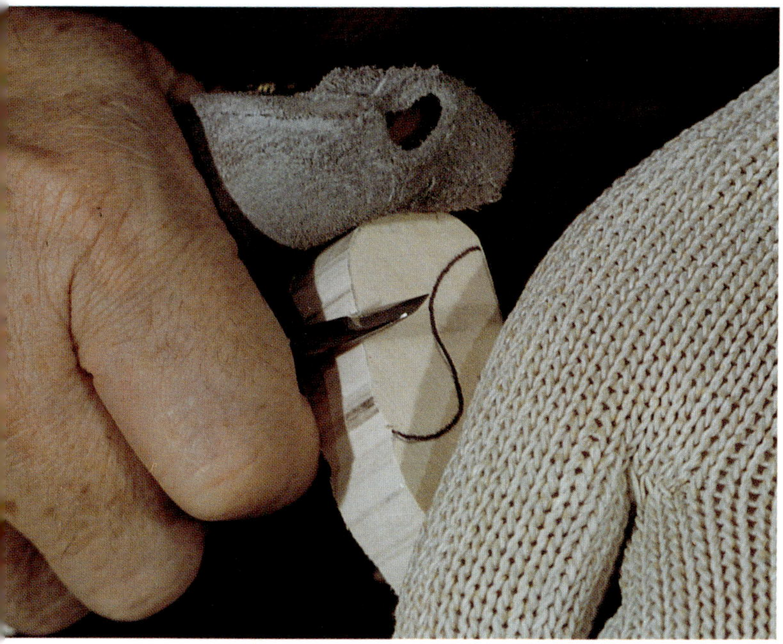

SAFETY TIP #2: **Protect your non-carving hand and fingers by wearing a carving glove.** The glove provides good protection but should not be considered as absolute protection. Some gloves are made with Kevlar, Spectra, and stainless steel. You should clearly understand the manufacturer's instructions and cautions for their carving glove.

SAFETY TIP #3: **Wear a thumb guard.** This protects your thumb when the knife slips off the wood or you cut through the wood in the direction of the thumb. It provides no protection for your non-carving hand. It is a safe idea to wear a thumb guard with a carving glove. The thumb guard should not be considered absolute protection.

SAFETY TIP #4: **Carve with a sharp knife and gouges!** A dull knife or carving tool is dangerous, leaves scars and scratches on the wood, tears up details, and wears out the hand. A dull knife tends to slide or bounce off the wood. I'm using a strop to produce a razor edge on my knife.

SAFETY TIP #6: **Store your knives and tools properly. You should always keep knives and tools out of the reach of children!** A simple box with dividers works. You just do not want to reach into an unorganized box and contact the edge of a knife or gouge. Believe me, it hurts! You can use clear plastic hose as a simple holder for each carving tool and knife. You need to keep the sharp edge of the tools from banging against one another and dulling the edges. I made this holder for my knife and gouges, or you can build or buy...

SAFETY TIP #5: **Do not force the knife or carving tool through the wood.** I know this does not seem to make sense but there is a fine balance between letting the knife or carving tool do the work and forcing it to cut more wood than your hand strength, tool sharpness, and skill level allow. If you cannot push or pull the knife or tool smoothly through the wood, remove it from the cut and try again, this time attempting to remove less wood. In time, as the knife hand becomes stronger and more controlled, you should discover yourself removing more with each cut. Remember that wood carving is not an art form of strength (how much wood you can remove with each cut) but a patient effort of transforming a piece of wood into an object of beauty.

a case designed just for wood carving tools.

BASIC TOOLS OF WOOD CARVING

THE KNIFE

Woodcarving requires a sharp knife. Some carvers prefer to carve only with a knife. In FIRST PROJECTS, we encourage you to use additional carving tools along with the knife.

A sharp knife is the foundation tool of the wood carver. The knife becomes the extension of your eyes, hands, mind, and heart. It transfers your imagination, skills, and creativity to the wood.

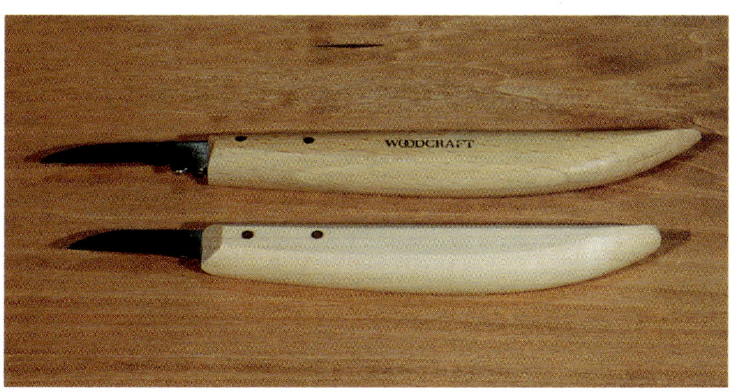

You have several options for knives. You can choose one like I started with, a bench knife. This style of knife remains extremely popular with carvers. For the FIRST PROJECTS in the book, you need a knife with a blade similar to the one on the bench knife. I recommend a blade length of approximately 1 1/2" inches for the FIRST PROJECTS. I have found that the shorter the blade, the more control. When you purchase a knife, ask the supplier if the knife is sharp and ready to use or if it needs work on a sharpening device such as a stone, diamond hone and strop. Some suppliers offer sharpening services. I encourage you to try different knives and blade styles. In most carving projects, it can be helpful to have more than one knife. Experimentation and experience help you select the best knife blade for your carvings.

You can choose a replaceable blade knife. The blades are usually razor sharp and available in a variety of sizes and shapes.

You can choose a custom knife and can expect to pay from $20 to $75 each. Most come with a blade that is usually razor sharp and ready to use.

CARVING TOOLS

Besides a sharp knife, you need to consider purchasing a few additional carving tools. They allow you to make cuts that would be difficult or time consuming with only a knife.

The most common woodcarving tools include chisels, gouges, v-parting tools, and veiners. Additional tools include: bent gouges, spoon gouges, back-bent gouges, fishtail gouges, bent v-parting tools. The tools vary in shape, styles, and size with each producing a distinct cut in the wood. European made gouges are sized in metric and American tools in inches. Each tool has a number that tells the curve or "sweep" of the blade. A No. 3 sweep is almost straight while a No. 11 is "U" shaped. The tools range from micro size to palm size to full size.

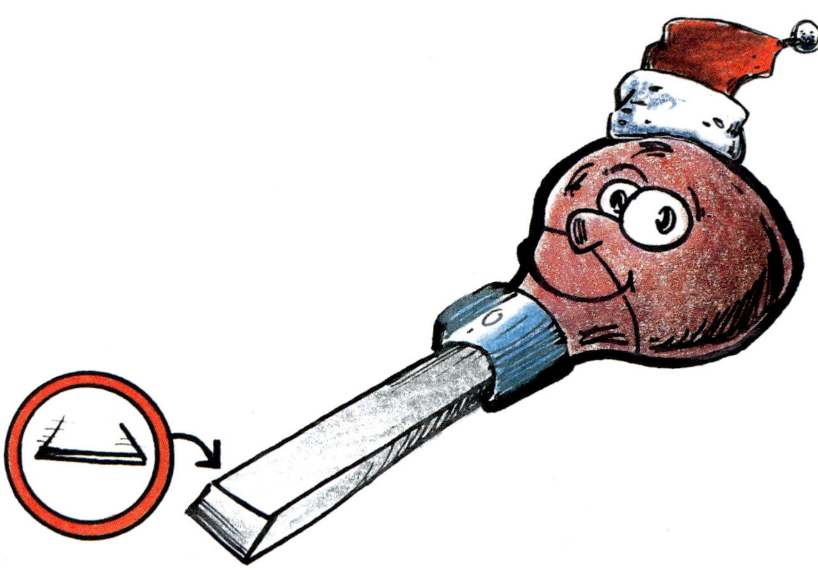

Chisel: A flat tool beveled on both sides. The carver's chisel has both sides beveled where a wood working chisel has only one side beveled. Woodcarving chisels are available in straight or skew design.

Gouges: A tool with a curved blade. Gouges can range in size from 1mm to over 70mm. Use one for roughing out a carving and adding details where curved surfaces are needed.

V-Parting Tool: Commonly called a v-tool. The tool has straight sides and a vee at the bottom edge. Use a v-tool for adding detail, setting an outline, and adding decorations and texture, such as hair or a beard.

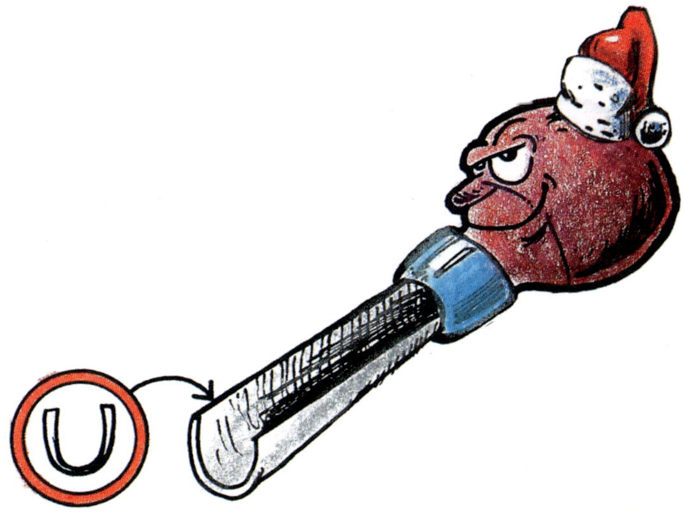

Veiners: They are U-shaped in construction. A veiner differs from a gouge in that a veiner's sides extend above a semi-circle, thus allowing you to make deep round cuts in the wood.

Advice on which tools, sizes, and how many to purchase will vary depending on with whom you talk and what you plan to carve. Since this book focuses on the new carver, we suggest the purchase of palm carving tools. If you plan to carve larger projects, we suggest you find a carver and discuss tools for larger projects with him or her. You can purchase a set of palm carving tools, or buy one or two tools at a time and add to your collection as you progress with carving. Palm carving tools come in various handle shapes, sweeps, and sizes. Pictured is a set of Swiss made tools. I thank Woodcraft Supply, of Parkersburg, West Virginia, for these tools.

The Flexcut ™ palm carving tools have a unique design. They feature a spring shank that can change shape as the contour of the wood dictates. In addition, the tool has an ergonomically designed handle.

All carvers have favorite sizes and shapes of carving tools. Their favorites are chosen based on the type of carving they do, the "feel" of the tool, performance, and ability to hold a sharp edge. What might be just right for someone else might not be just right for you. Tom Brown, a member of Caricature Carvers of America, suggests a set of palm carving tools for carvers that allows one to tackle most small to medium size projects. We want to thank Larry Yudis at The Woodcraft Shop in Bettendorf, Iowa for supplying the palm carving tools. Tom's six favorite tools are (from left to right) a 5/32" V-parting tool, 3/16" No. 11 veiner, 5/16" V-parting tool, 3/8" No. 9 gouge, 1/2" No. 3 fish tail gouge, and a 3/4" No. 3 gouge.

HELPFUL ITEMS USED IN WOOD CARVING

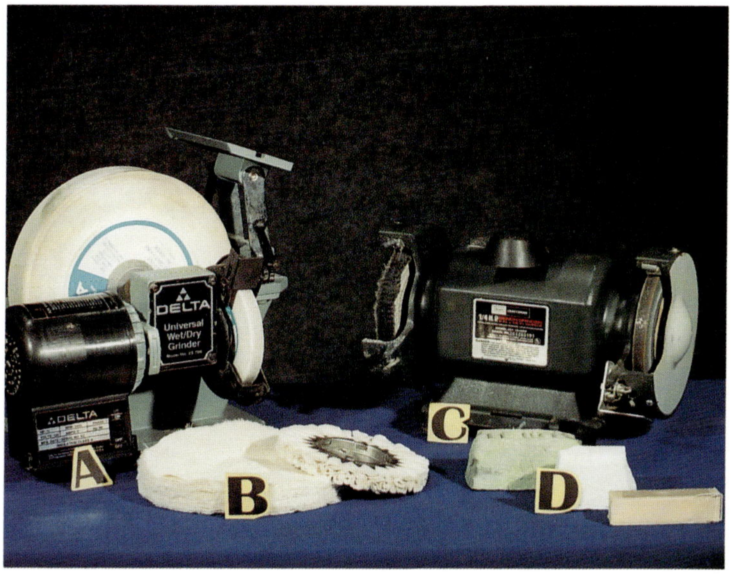

There are several power aids designed for sharpening. We encourage you to talk with an experienced carver who uses these aids. A) **Wet/Dry Grinder:** a grinder that features a water wheel; B) **Buffing Wheel:** a cloth wheel that mounts on a bench grinder. Other wheel materials such as leather or felt can be used; C) **Bench Grinder:** a tool to which a buffing wheel and sharpening stone are attached; D) **Buffing Compound:** an abrasive substance which is applied to a buffing wheel or strop to help produce a razor edge on a knife or gouge. Some popular compounds are Yellowstone, Zam, and jewelers rouge.

Eye punches: A circle punch which, when pushed into the wood and rotated, produces the round curved surface of an eye, button, or various details.

Besides a knife and carving tools, there are several helpful items you can use. We have selected a few and given a short explanation of each.

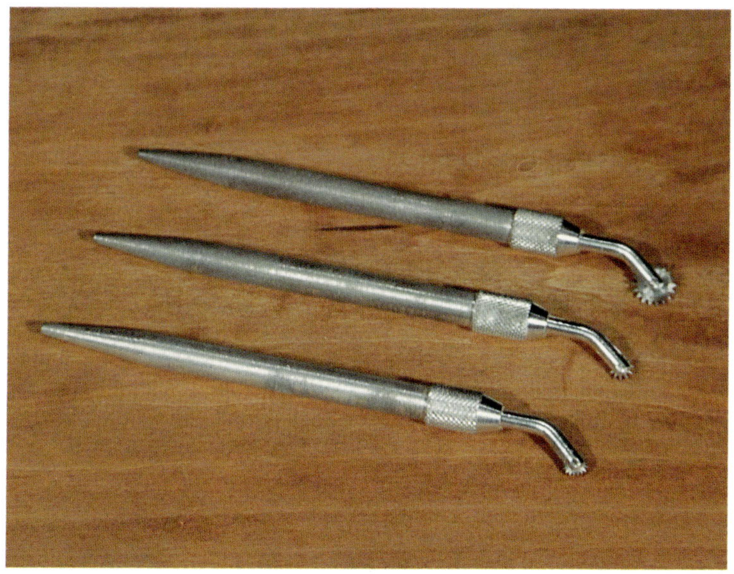

Pounce wheels: tools that can be used to add stitching to boots and clothes. I want to thank Smoky Mountain Woodcarvers Supply in Townsend, Tennessee for providing the pounce wheels.

Flexible shaft tool: a high RPM rotary tool used for detailing, drilling, general shaping, and roughing. A) flexible shaft handles usually allow for interchange of tools. I have a carbide burr in mine B) tungsten carbide burrs, C) sanding cones and drums, and (not pictured) drills.

Strop: a tool used for the final step of the sharpening process. It is constructed of wood with a layer of leather attached. The leather is treated with an abrasive compound such as Yellowstone or Zam.

Sharpening Stone: an abrasive stone used to sharpen knives and gouges. The stones are classed according to their abrasiveness (grit) and are either natural or synthetic. Some of the popular natural stones are India, Washita, Soft Arkansas and Hard Arkansas. Another type of sharpening stone is an EZE-LAPE™ Diamond Hone & Stone. The smaller stone is a round slipstone and is used on the inside of gouges. Slipstones also come in tapered triangles, knife edge, rounds, and points.

Woodburner: an electrical tool used to burn details into wood. The woodburner usually has interchangeable tips. I thank my good friends at Woodcraft Supply in Parkersburg, West Virginia for the Swiss made palm carving tools, flexible shaft tool, and the woodburner.

WOOD

What is the best type of wood for carving? Basswood (linden) is the preferred wood for most carvers. It is a hardwood with dense grain that lends itself to details. Basswood usually is free of knots. Other woods for most projects include buckeye, butternut, sugar or white pine, and walnut. Duck and bird carvers seem to prefer tupelo and juletong.

SHARPENING THE TOOLS

To have an enjoyable experience in carving, you need sharp tools! The quality of the blade steel, how it is sharpened, how you use it, the kind of wood you're carving, and the amount of carving, determine how long a knife stays sharp. **A dull knife or carving tool is dangerous, leaves scars and scratches on the wood, tears up details, and wears out your hand.** There are as many different approaches to sharpening as there are carvers. If you want to get a conversation started, ask a carver how he or she sharpens tools! Go to another carver and you will probably get a different answer.

This book is not the authority on sharpening. We believe the quickest method for sharpening is through the use of power equipment. We realize, however, that you may not have the space, interest, or readiness to invest in the necessary power equipment. It is important to gain an overview of the fundamentals. We are sharing what has worked for us.

You need to remember what I call the three "P's" of sharpening. **Number 1: Patience:** Do not be in a hurry. The extra time you spend sharpening/honing can eliminate dull tools, tired hands and maybe even a cut. **Number 2: Position:** You need to understand the proper position/angle of the tools on the stone, strop or buffing wheel. Without the correct angle you can end up dulling or damaging your tools. We recommend you keep the knife flat on the stone and strop. **Number 3: Practice:** Like carving, sharpening is going to take some practice. Most things we attempt we get better at through practice. However, if you find that you just cannot get your knife or gouges sharp, find a carver who is willing to help. Don't let your carving days end in frustration because you cannot get the tools sharp.

There are two important tasks involved in preparing and maintaining your tools for carving. They are sharpening and honing. You also need to understand two important terms that are associated with these tasks. They are wire edge and bevel.

What is a wire edge? It is sometimes called a "burr." Through sharpening, the metal edge becomes thin and curls up on the top of the blade. The wire edge appears on the side facing up from the stone. It does not form on the side of the blade against the stone. This wire edge signals that a new edge has developed. The thickness would be thinner than aluminum foil.

The knives show two types of bevels. On the left is a short bevel (which is usually found on most new unsharpened carving knives) and on the right a long bevel. Tom, Mac, and I prefer knives and carving tools with long bevels. They cut through the wood easier. If you purchase a knife or gouge with a short bevel, we suggest you consider extending the bevel. The short bevel is primarily for working in hardwood such as walnut or oak. The longer bevel is more suited for work in woods such as basswood and buckeye. Changing the bevel on a tool is accomplished with a stone. Power equipment can do the work quicker, but will require more skill and practice. Before trying to change the bevel on a knife or gouge, we suggest you locate a woodcarver who has experience in this area. His or her experience can help you eliminate mistakes.

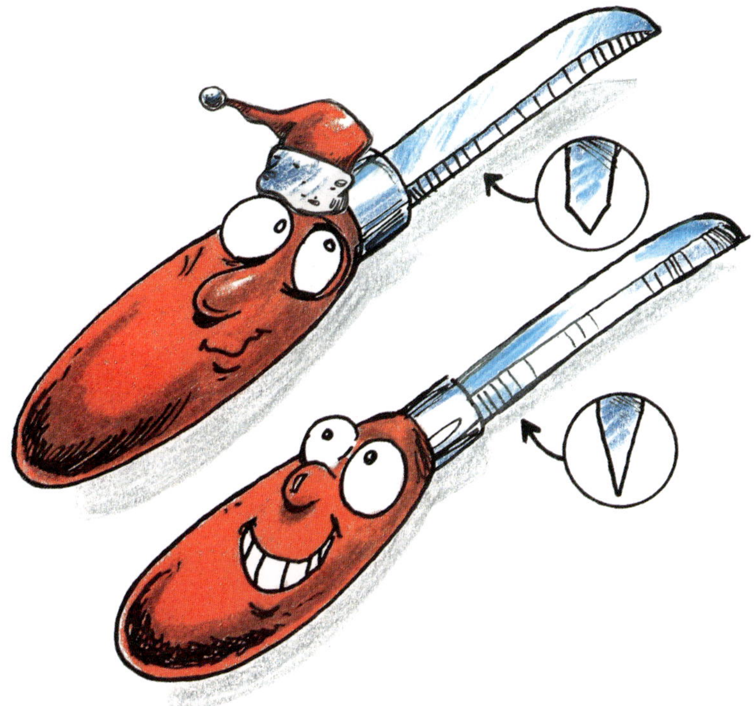

TASK ONE: SHARPENING. **Use this step if the knife or gouge is new (unsharpened), damaged, dull, or is in need of the blade bevel being changed.** Sharpening requires the use of a stone (Hard Arkansas or similar stone, Diamond hone, or power device). You need to follow the manufacturer's instructions for the use and care of a stone. Sharpening produces a wire edge on the cutting edge.

To obtain a wire edge, place the knife flat on the stone with the sharp edge facing away from you. Exert pressure on the blade and pull the knife toward you. Take a few strokes and check for the wire edge. It must appear on the length of the blade. **Most new carvers do not continue the sharpening process until the wire edge appears.** Continue this action repeatedly until the wire edge appears on the side of the knife, facing up. Some carvers use a magnifying glass to check for the wire edge. Others use light and allow it to reflect on the blade and see the wire edge by this means. The wire edge is not a flat surface so light does not reflect off it. The wire edge needs to form the complete length of the blade. Remember the 3 P's: Patience, Position, and Practice.

Obtaining a wire edge during the sharpening process applies to gouges and v-tools as well. However, you must rotate the edge of the tool from side to side across the stone for a gouge. You only produce a wire edge on the inside of a gouge or v-tool. For a v-tool, you must work the tool so you maintain the vee at the bottom. The v-tool is the most difficult to sharpen. Care must be used not to sharpen one side more than the other. We suggest you seek the assistance of an experienced carver for the v-tool.

After you have produced a wire edge on one side, turn the knife on the other side and work to produce a wire edge. As you work on this side, the wire edge from the other side will eventually curl up on the side facing up. Exert pressure on the blade and push the knife away from you with the sharp edge facing toward you. Continue this action repeatedly until a wire edge appears on the cutting edge. When it appears on this side, you are finished with this step.

TASK TWO: HONING. **Use this step on a knife or gouge to remove the wire edge formed by the stone and fine scratches left by the stone. Once a knife is sharp you can use this step to maintain a razor edge.** If the blade has been sharpened properly, you should **only need** to return to the stone if you break or chip the blade or if you wish to change the shape of the blade. Honing is accomplished with a fine grit stone and a strop. Each time you start to carve, give the knife blade a few licks on the strop to maintain the razor edge. This also will remove any moisture that may have collected on the blade through storage. **When you're carving, it is a good idea to periodically use the strop to maintain the edge.**

Hone with a fine grit stone and a strop. You can use a fine grit stone to remove scratches left by a more abrasive stone. I use a 3000 grit stone for the honing process and then finish with a strop. To use a strop, spread the abrasive compound on the strop. I am using Yellowstone. I just scrape it off the block onto the strop.

Place the knife flat and keep it flat on the strop, with the sharp edge facing away from you. While exerting pressure on the blade (this helps keep the blade flat), pull the knife toward you and then turn the knife over and push it away from you. Continue going in both directions until you have removed the wire edge and any scratches left by the stone, and have produced a mirror finish on the blade. Remember the 3 P's: Patience, Position, and Practice.

A gouge is honed by rotating it from side to side along the strop, keeping it flat along the bevel.

Use a round edge slipstone or piece of leather to remove the wire edge from inside the gouge.

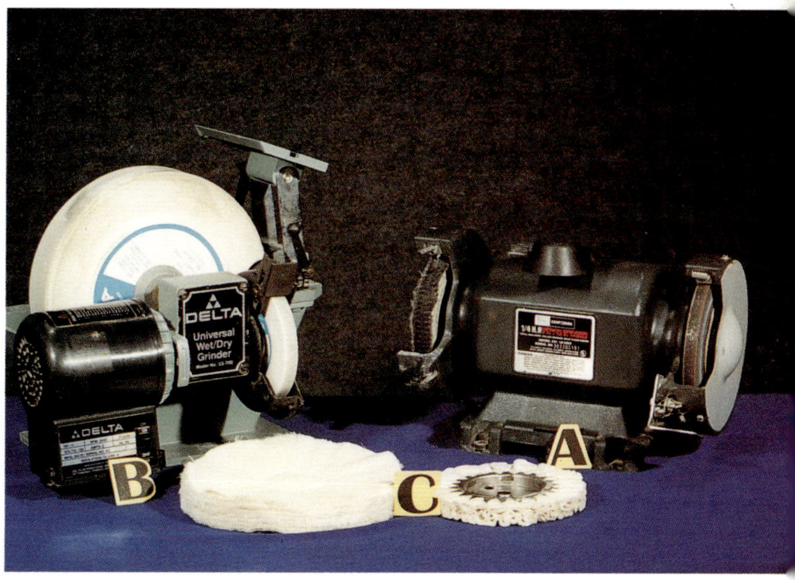

To speed up the sharpening/honing process, you may want to consider investing in power equipment designed for sharpening and honing. The photo shows a small sample of the many products available. A) **Bench grinder:** a tool to which a buffing wheel and sharpening stone are attached. B) **Wet/Dry grinder:** a grinder that features a water wheel. C) **Buffing wheel:** a cloth wheel that mounts on a bench grinder. Other wheel materials such as leather or felt can be used. Consult an experienced carver who is familiar with power assisted sharpening before investing in this equipment. Proper safety techniques must be utilized with the equipment.

KNIFE PRACTICE

This section can help you become familiar with the knife and some basic cuts you will be making in FIRST PROJECTS and on future carvings. Different carvers might call these cuts by other names. There does not appear to be a consensus on the terms. You will find yourself repeating these cuts again and again. The best way to teach you is to show the cuts and then for you to practice on a scrap piece of wood. **I strongly suggest you use a carving glove and thumb guard for these practice cuts. For purposes of illustration, I am not carving with a thumb guard in some of the pictures so you can better see the position of my thumb.**

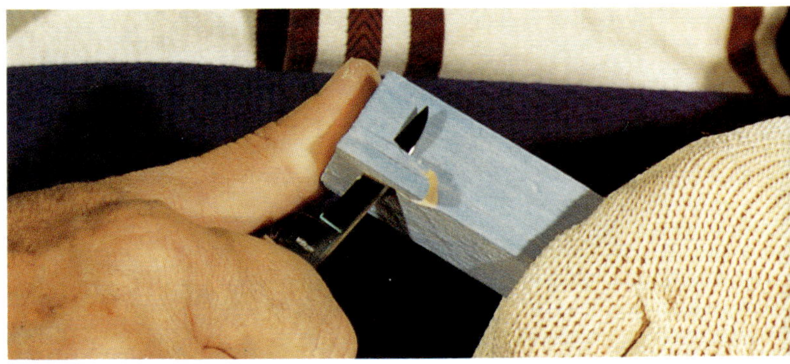

THE PULL CUT: This is the workhorse cut of carving. You can use this cut to do most of the wood removal and shaping on a project. It's like making a fist over and over. Maintain a firm grip on the practice wood. You do not want it slipping out of your hands. Place your thumb below the path of the knife. Place the knife in the wood and gently pull the blade toward the end/edge of the wood. **Keep the thumb out of the path of the knife. If you have a thumb guard, I suggest you use it.** Make several cuts completely around the wood. Vary the starting point of the knife. This will give you a "feel" of how it requires more strength to pull the knife the farther away it is from your thumb. Vary the depth of the cut until you find the depth that feels most comfortable. DO NOT FORCE THE KNIFE. If it does not pull smoothly through the wood you need to stop and attempt a shallower cut.

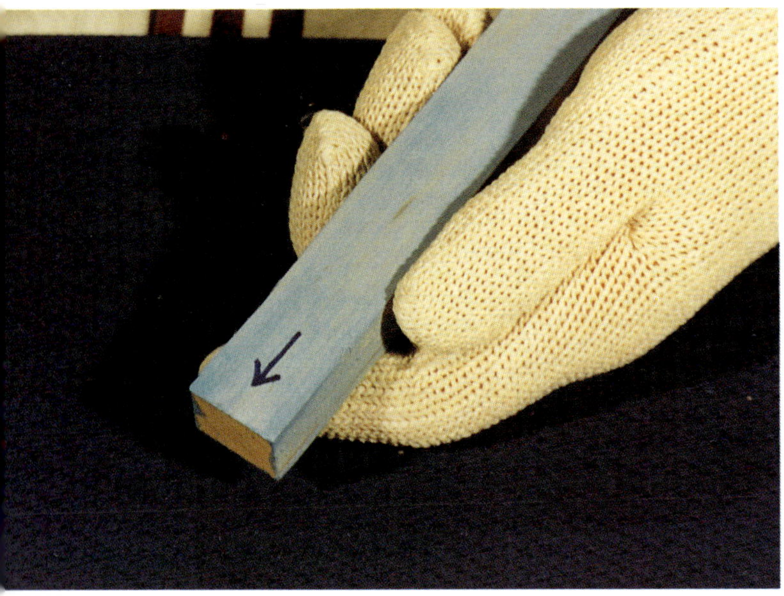

I am using a piece of basswood 8" long, 3/4" thick, and 1" wide. The arrow shows the grain running the length of the piece. You can use whatever size you have available. Just make sure it is large enough so you can get a good hold. If you cannot find basswood, I suggest you use sugar or white pine. I discourage the use of yellow pine used for shelves and 2 x 4's. It contains sap and knots that can dull the tools, plus it's just plain hard to carve. However, if yellow pine is all you can find then you have to use what you have. I have painted my practice board with a blue wash to help the cuts stand out. You do not need to do this to yours.

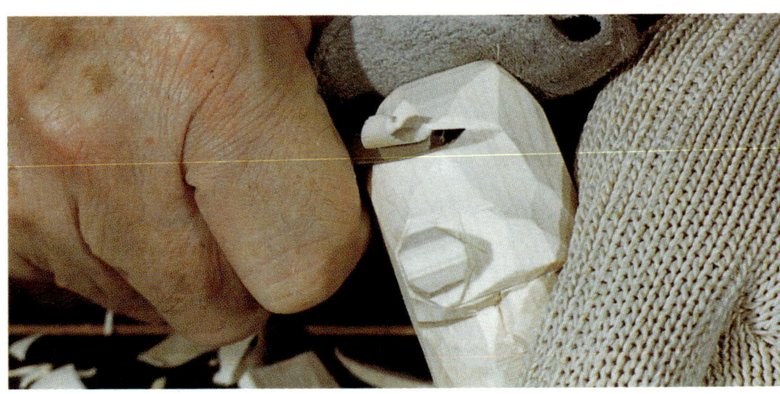

The PULL CUT in action on the Santa.

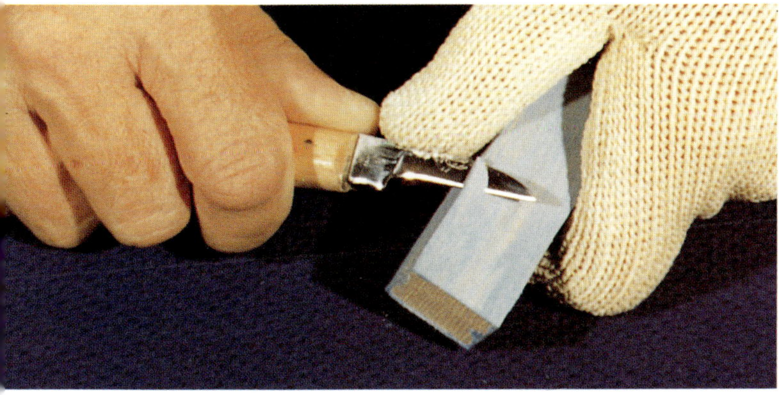

THE PUSH CUT or CONTROLLED CUT: This cut is used when the direction of the grain or location of the cut will not allow you to use the pull cut. This cut requires a little more coordination of the hands. Place the knife on the wood and place the other thumb on the back of the blade or on the back of your thumb on the knife hand. While firmly holding the wood, exert pressure on the back of the blade, thus pushing the knife through the wood. Work your way around the practice wood. Vary the depth and length of cut. DO NOT FORCE THE KNIFE.

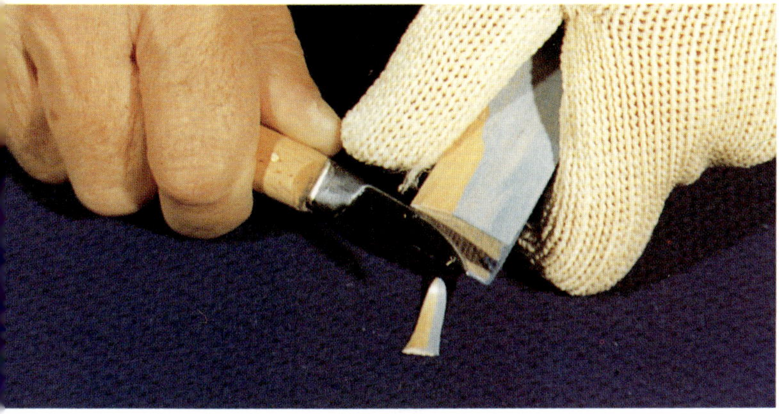

The PUSH CUT completed. Repeat the cut several times until you feel comfortable.

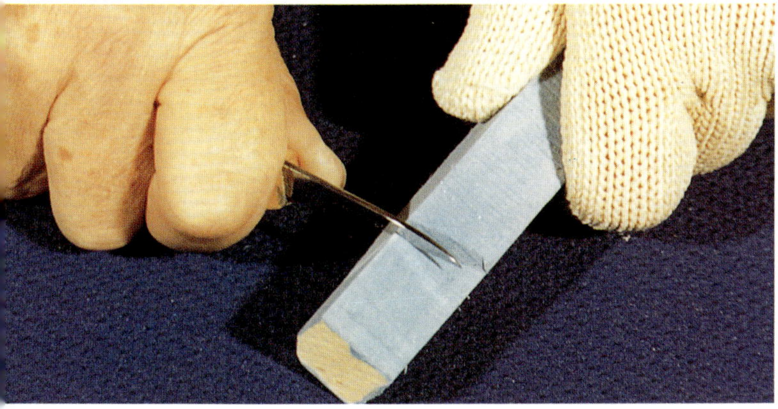

THE STOP CUT: Use this cut to control the movement of the knife, v-tool, or gouge through the wood. It is a two step cut. You can use this cut when shaping or detailing a particular feature on a project. **Step 1**: Place the knife on the wood and push in firmly. This is a stop cut! It can also be made with just the point of the knife cutting into the wood. This is called **incising.**

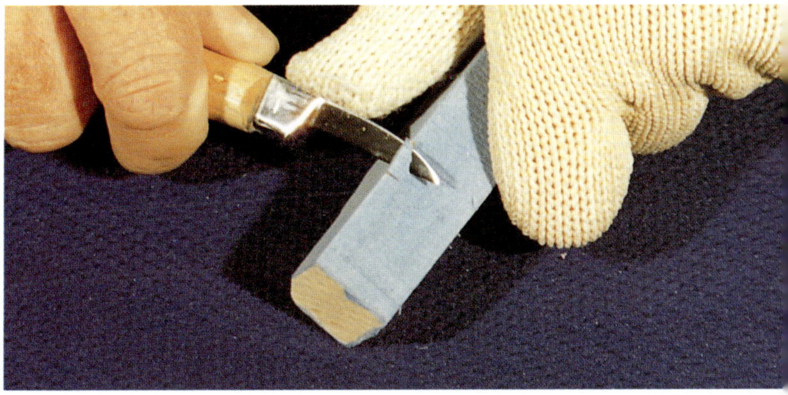

Step 2: Place the knife on the wood, adjust the angle of the blade to match the depth you want to cut, and slowly use the push cut to move the knife blade into the stop cut. In some situations, you might use the pull cut to cut back to a stop cut. The piece of wood should pop loose. The angle of the knife needs to match the depth of the stop cut at the point where the two cuts intersect.

The push cut being made toward a stop cut on the Christmas stocking. Notice how my thumb is exerting pressure on the back of my other thumb.

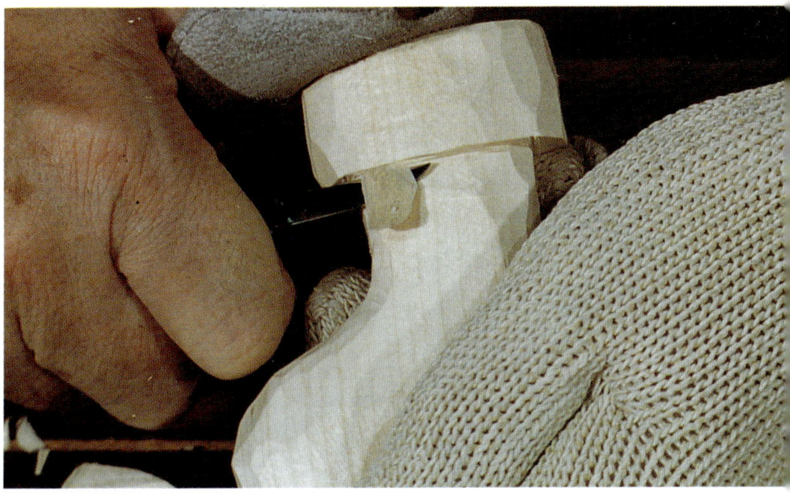

The pull cut being made toward a stop cut on the Christmas stocking. This combination of cuts sets the cuff of the stocking away from the body of the stocking.

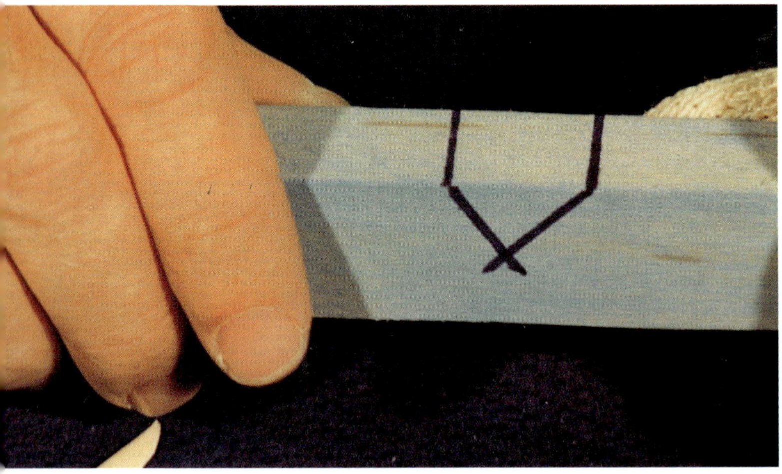

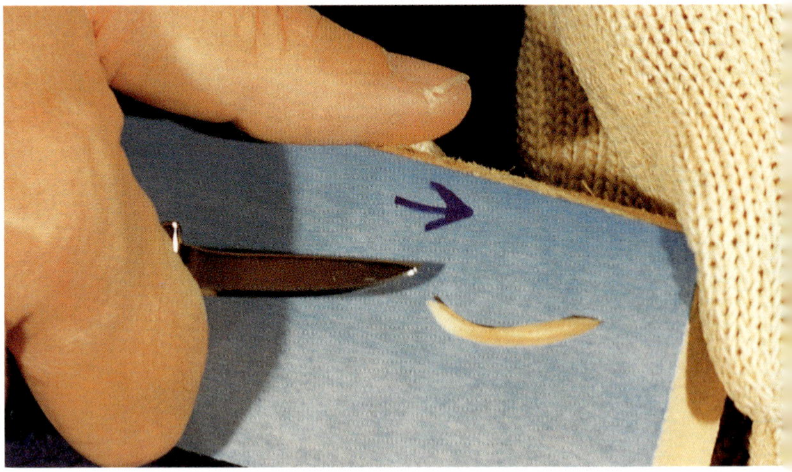

THE LINE CUT: This is a two step cut. Use the LINE CUT to remove wood where you want to reset or separate the wood between two areas. The cut can be used to define the separation between an arm and the body or a coat and shirt, anywhere details come together that you want to separate. I drew this large so you can see how the two cuts should overlap.

The completed cut.

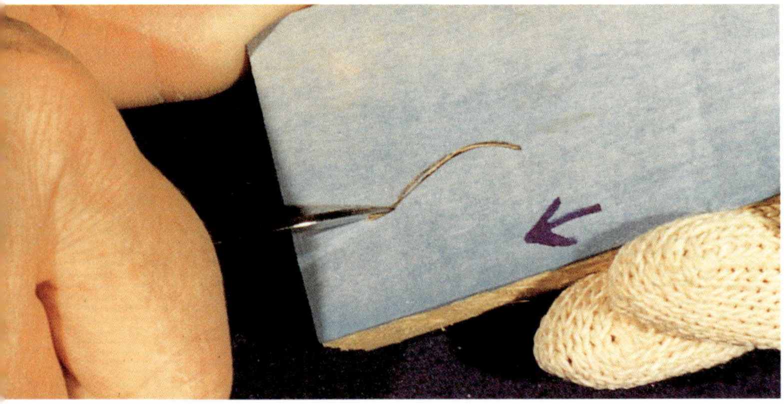

Make a cut at an angle along the surface of the practice wood.

THE PYRAMID CUT: This is a three step cut. The three sides will not always be the same length. It is a combination of cuts made in the shape of a triangle. Use the pyramid cut to remove wood from such areas as the corner of an eye, to recess a mouth, to add detail to clothing, to add wrinkles next to a belt. You can find several uses for this cut and in most cases not even be aware you are using it. **You need to draw several small triangles on your board**. So you can see better, we have made a large triangle. Tom Brown is demonstrating a pyramid cut in the photos below.

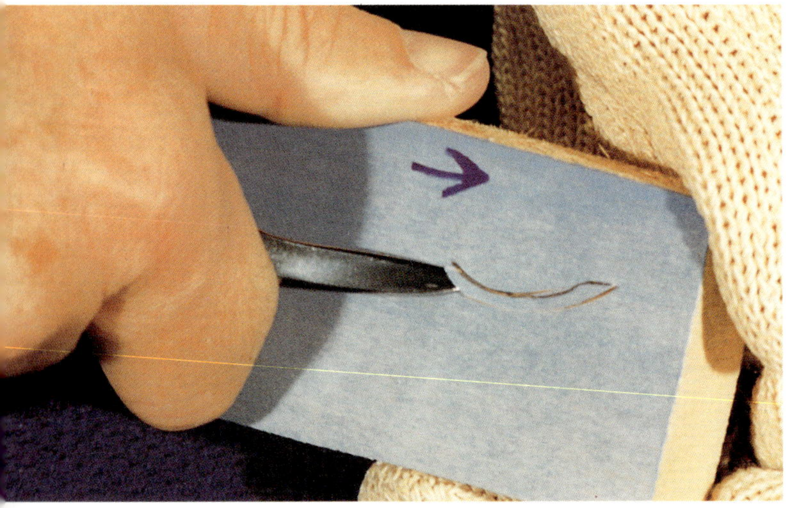

Rotate the wood and follow the line with the same angle and depth of cut. It is important to rotate the wood so the knife is at the correct angle and position for the cut. The wood should pop out.

Make a deep cut at a slight angle along one edge of the triangle.

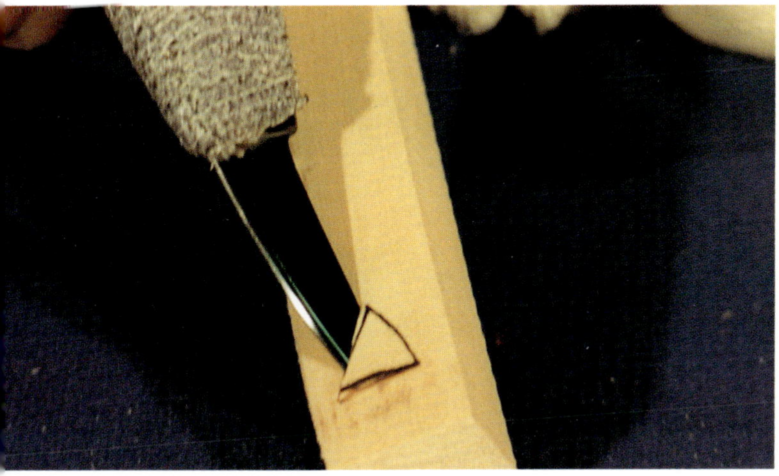

Make a second cut along the second side of the triangle. It does not matter which side.

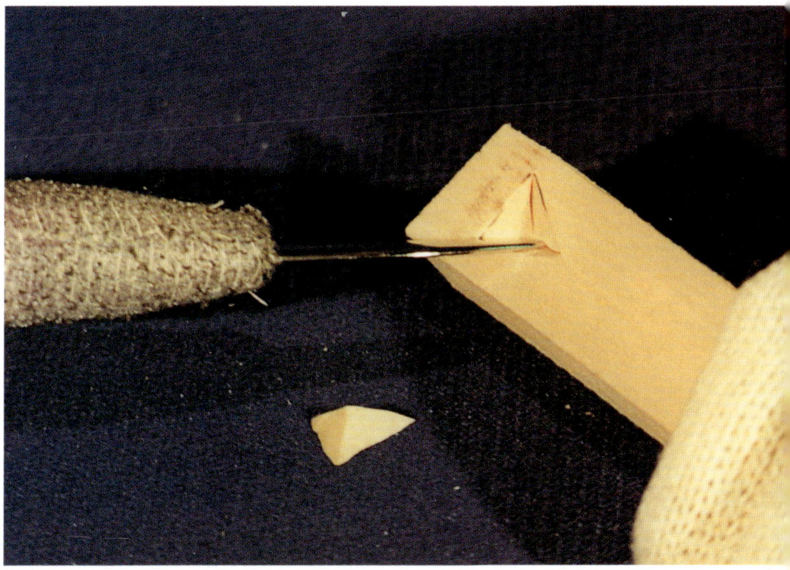

If the knife angle and depth have been correct, the pyramid should pop out just like Tom's.

Make a third cut along the third side.

This aviator was carved by Tom Brown; the mouth shows a perfect example of a pyramid cut.

GOUGE PRACTICE

With a gouge, v-tool, or veiner you can make cuts and details that are difficult with a knife. Since we will be using palm carving tools for our FIRST PROJECTS we will practice with one. You should always keep your non-carving hand out of the path of the carving tool.

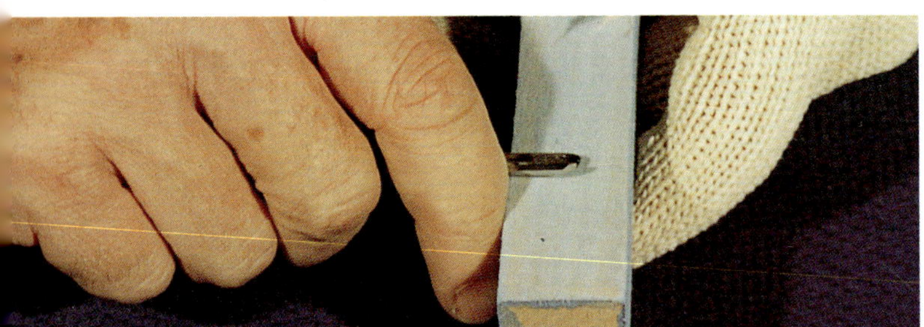

I prefer to hold the palm tool so my fingers act as a stop/brake to prevent the tool from racing wildly across the wood. You can see how the finger restricts or slows the movement. When you're carving, you should discover ways to use your fingers to restrict the movement of the gouge through the wood. You have much better control of the palm tool this way.

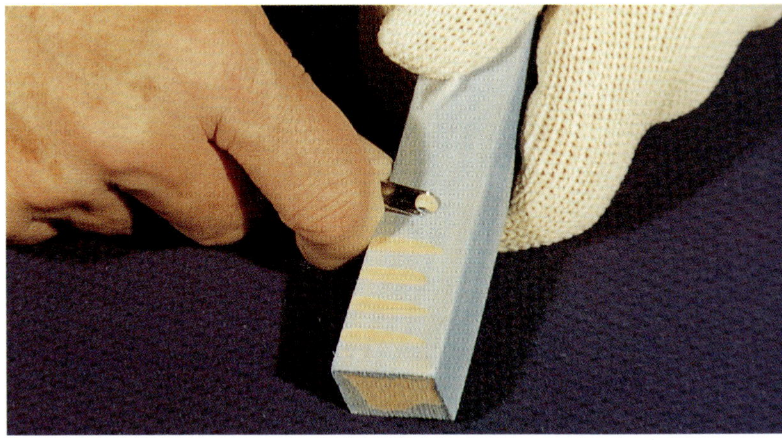

Practice pushing the gouge through the wood. Vary the depth and direction as you work your way down the board. During this practice session, you can tell if the gouges are sharp. If they do not cut smoothly or tear the wood, you need to do some more work on them.

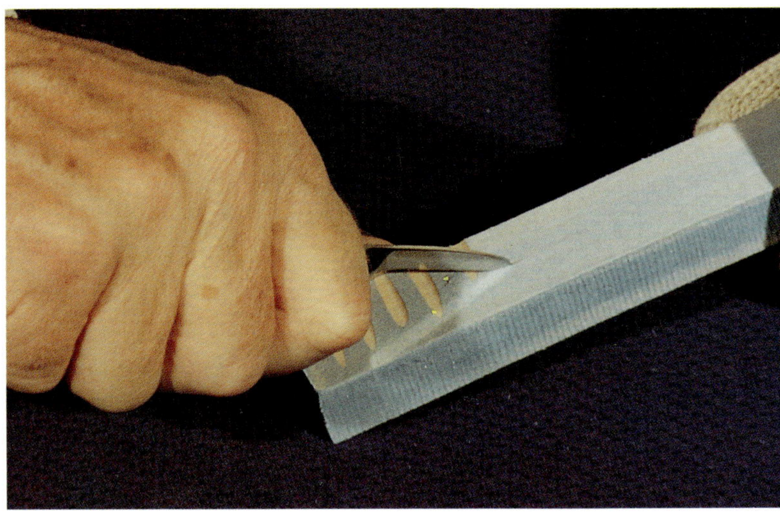

Use the knife to make a stop cut in the middle of the board.

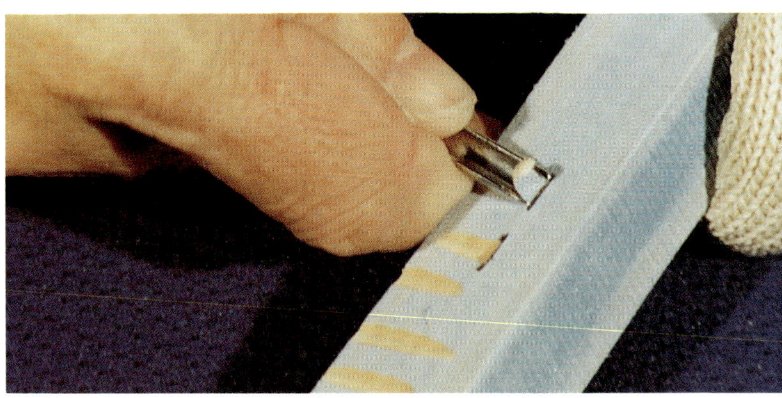

Push your tool up to the line stopping at the cut. Easy? The wood should pop out if the stop cut was deep enough to match the depth of the gouge cut. Continue to practice until you feel comfortable with the tools.

CHRISTMAS STOCKING

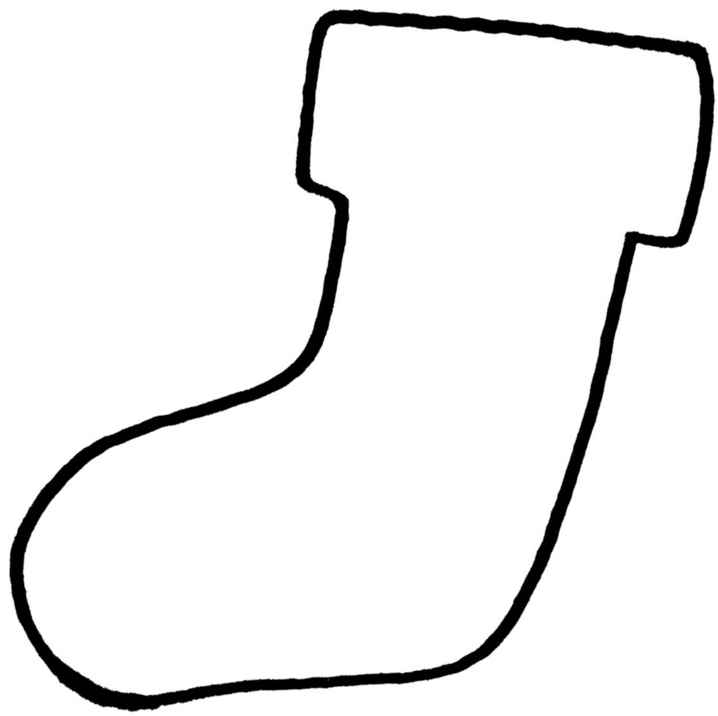

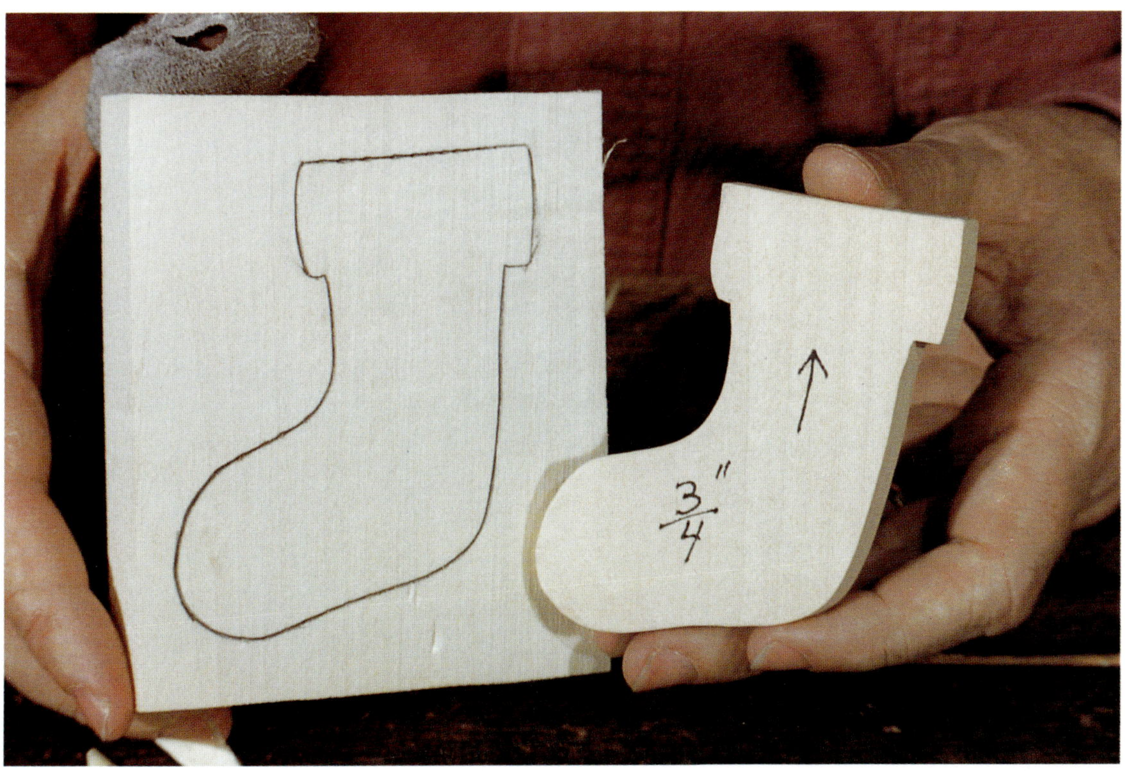

Use carbon paper to trace the stocking pattern on a 3/4" basswood board and then cut it out with a bandsaw or coping saw. **The grain runs from top to toe**. I make a thin wooden template to speed up the transfer of the pattern to the wood. This is especially helpful if you plan to carve several.

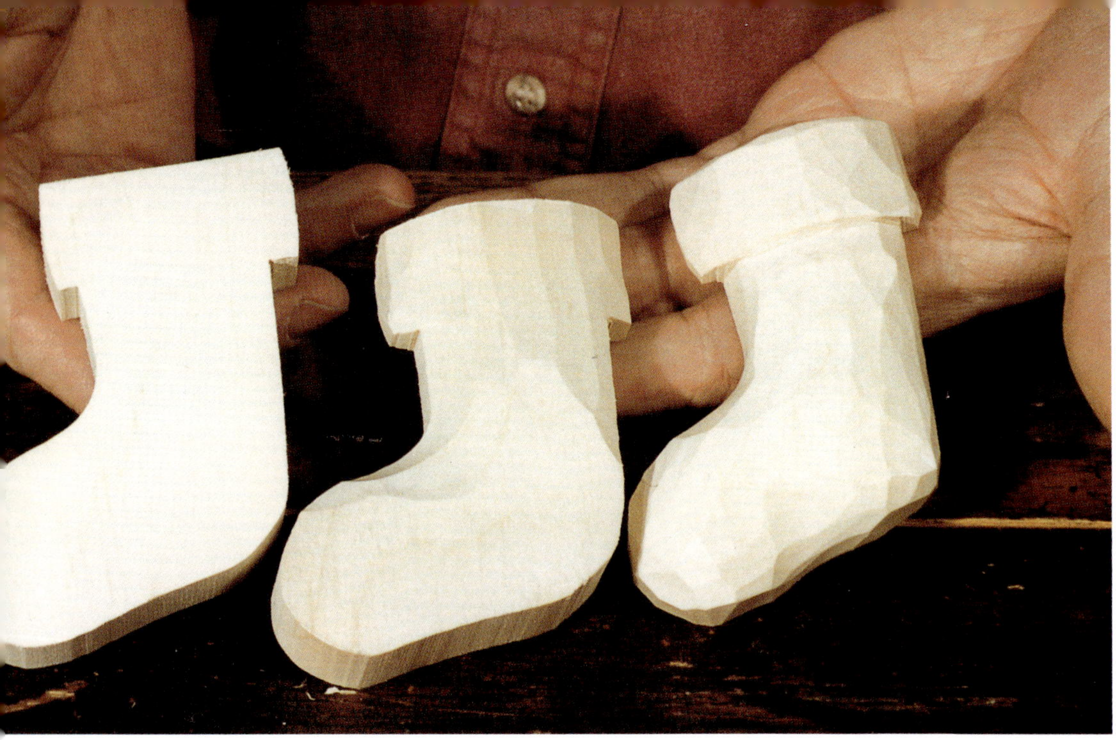

From left to right: the stocking blank, the stocking partially rounded and the completed stocking.

Draw a curve on the top. This line will determine the shape of the stocking top.

Draw a center line.

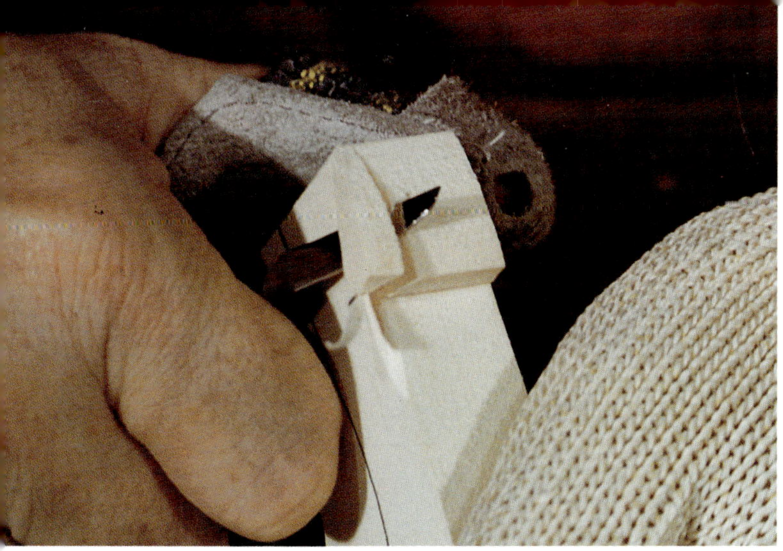

We are ready to make our first cut. I have put on a carving glove and thumb guard. I would encourage you to carve with these two safety aids. Remember, they are not absolute protection. Remove the wood from the edge of the stocking to the curved line on the top.

Continue to remove wood toward the center line. Don't cut into the curve line at the top.

The completed rounding on one side.

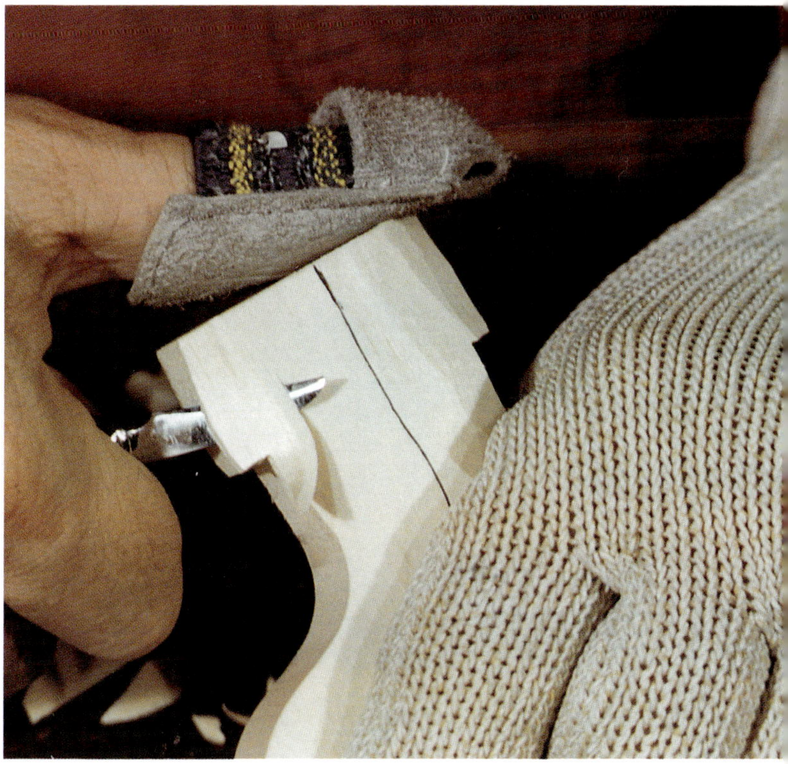

Repeat the rounding on the other side.

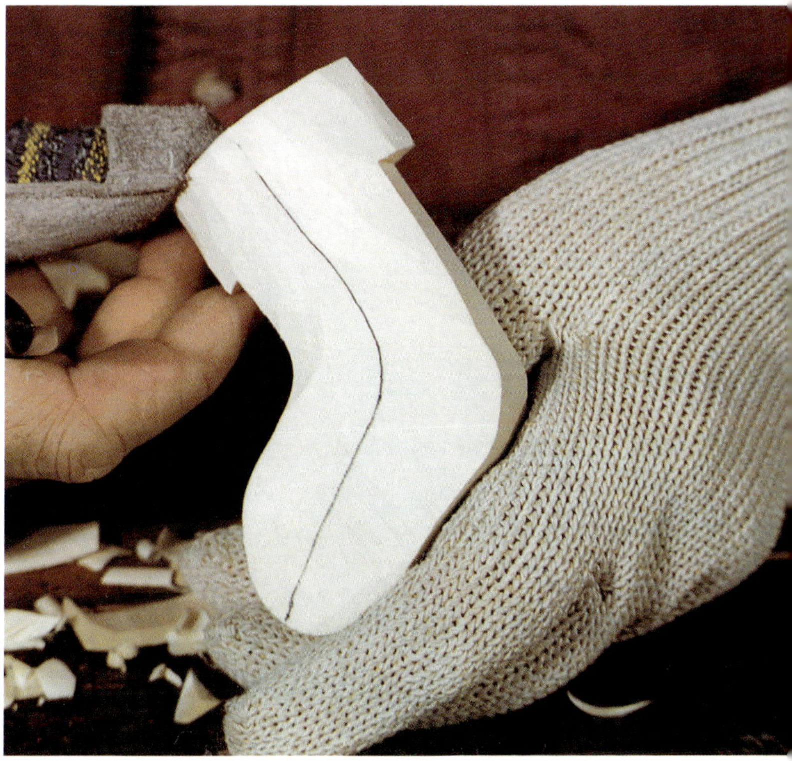

The completed rounding of the top.

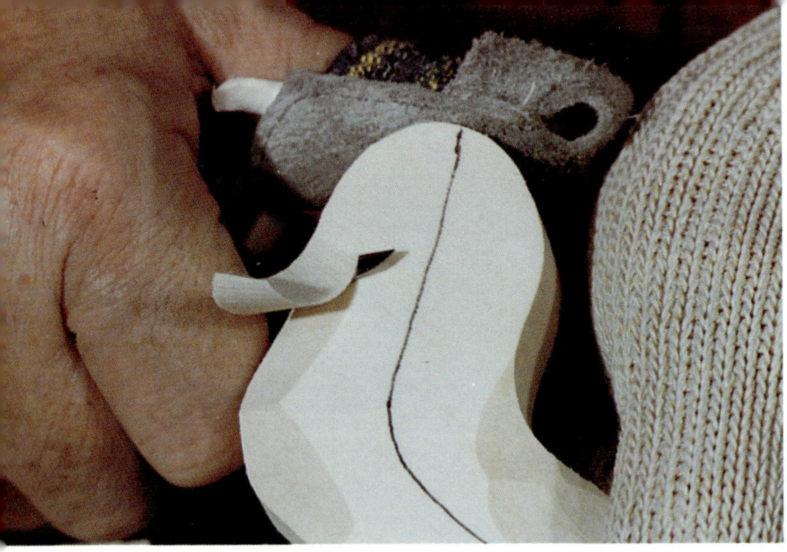

Remove some wood from the heel, working your way toward the toe.

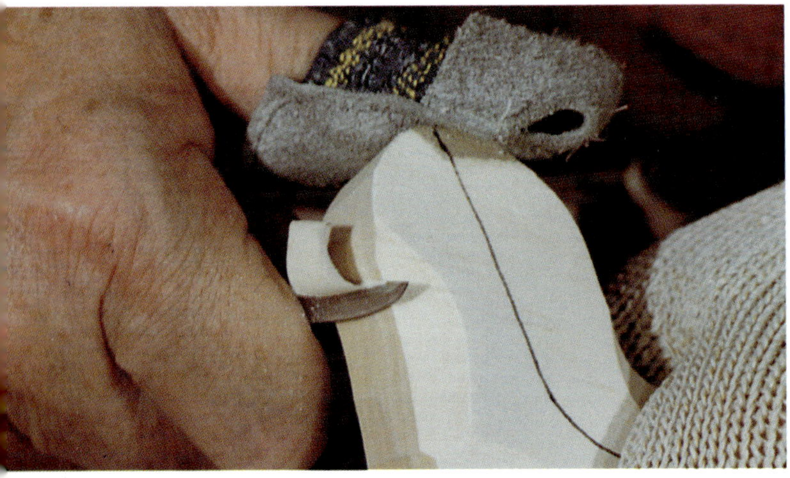

Remove the saw marks from the bottom.

Round the bottom of the stocking to the center line.

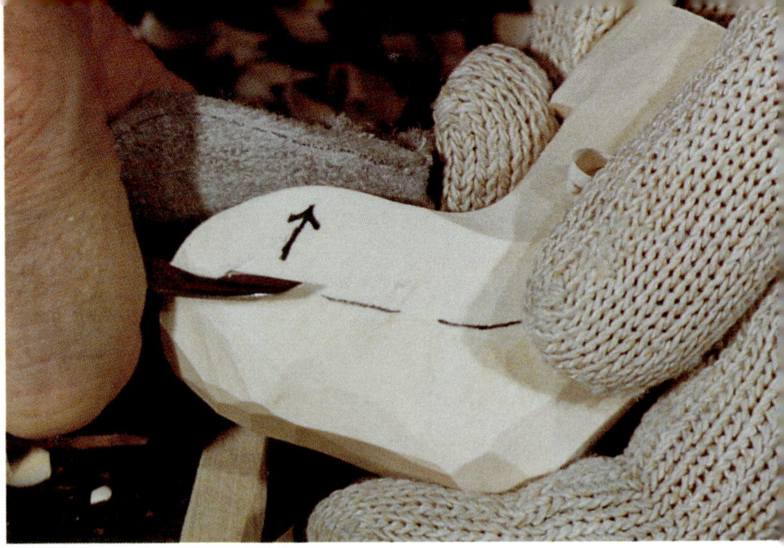

We are ready to round the top of the toe. The arrow indicates the direction of the grain. Your knife needs to cut above the center line in the direction of the arrow. Round the toe.

Continue to round the stocking toward the top. Remove wood toward the center line as you work your way up toward the folded down part. The whole stocking should have a rounded appearance.

Draw a line to separate the folded down part of the stocking from the lower part of the stocking. Incise the line creating a stop.

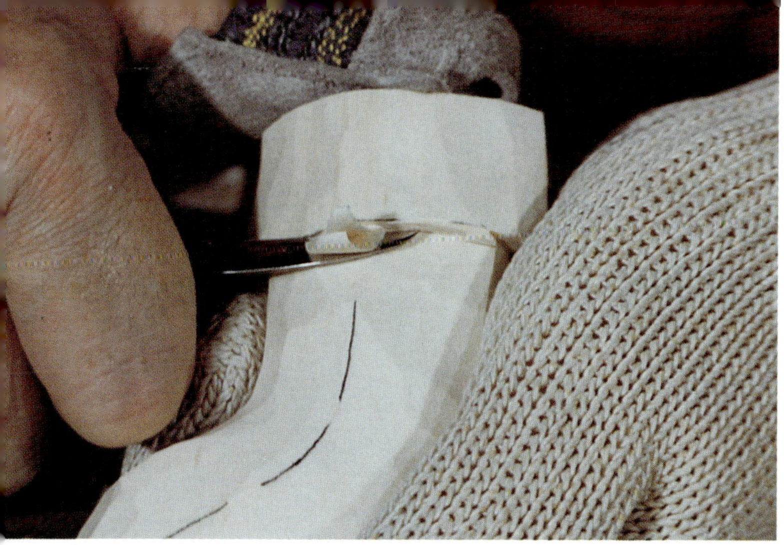

Remove wood back to the stop. I drop the lower part back about 1/8". I am using a pull cut.

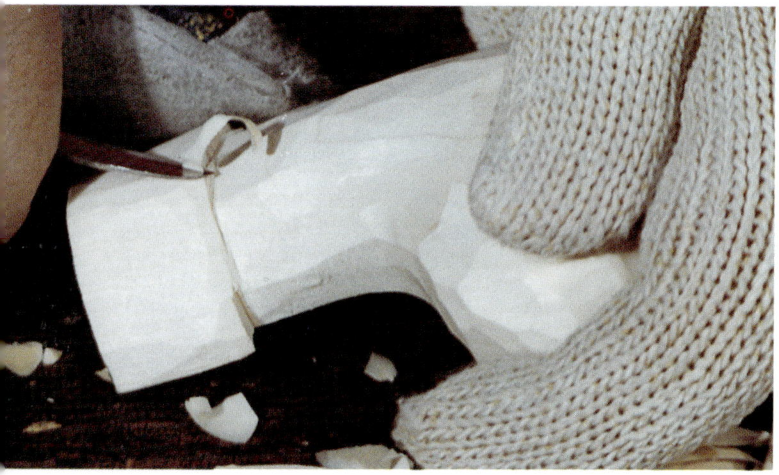

Round the bottom edge of the folded down part.

Draw the width of the top of the stocking and begin making scooping cuts toward the line. It is kind of like scooping ice cream out of a container. The goal is to drop the inside of the stocking away from the top.

This picture shows the completed scooping out of the top. Finish the top edge by removing the saw marks and rounding the edge.

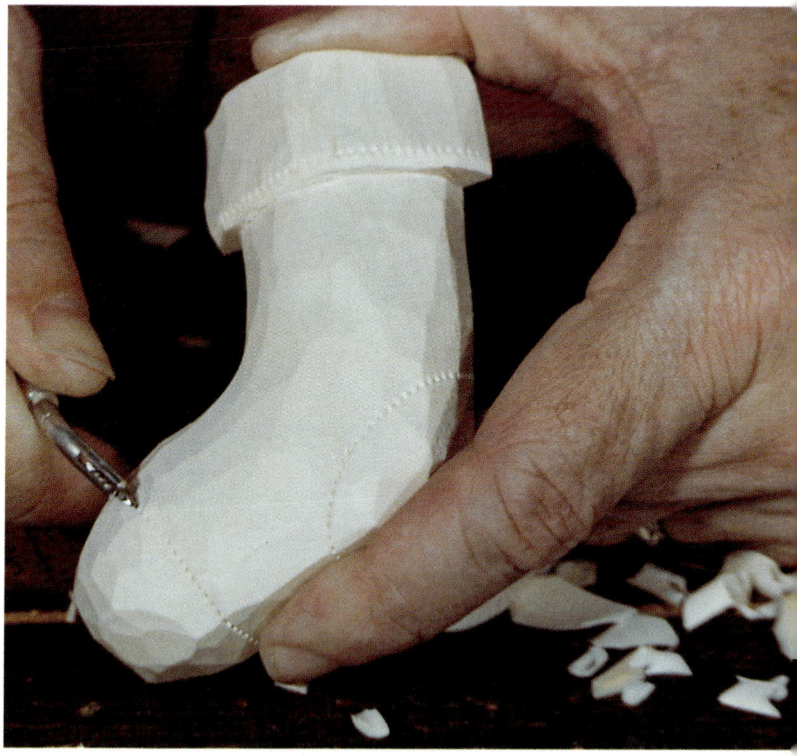

Use a pounce wheel to create patches on the toe and heel. I also run the wheel across the bottom edge of the folded over part. If you don't have a pounce wheel, you can use the point of your knife.

I use acrylic paints to finish the stocking. I want the stocking to have a bright look so I use the paint straight from the bottle. If I desire a lighter look, I dilute the paint with water to create a wash. Practice is the best teacher.

There are several options for finishing the stocking. You can paint a scene on it, add a name, add more decoration, experiment with different colors. Let your imagination rule. I like to use a wood burner to inscribe a name on the stocking. I am adding my son's name.

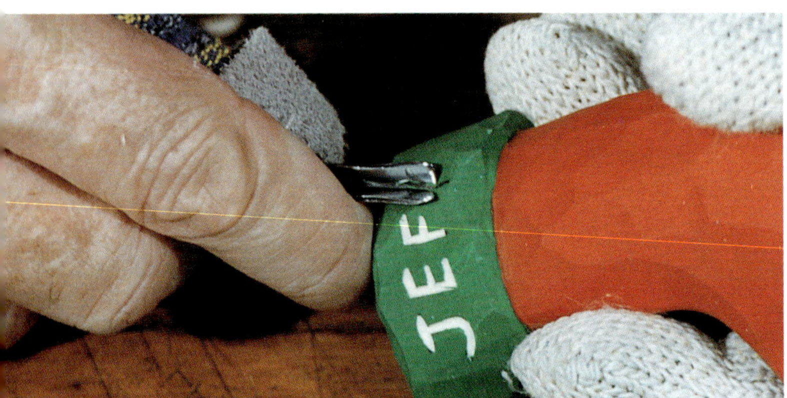

You can use a small v-tool to add a name.

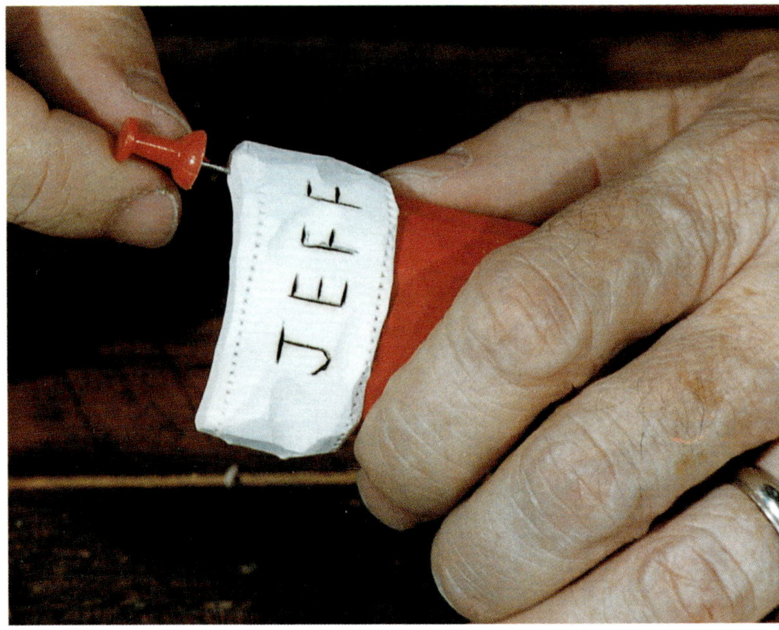

Since this is an ornament, we need to add an eyelet in which a Christmas ornament hanger can be inserted. I use a map pushpin to make a small hole for a screw eye.

Two completed stockings showing variations in the color and name finishes.

SNOWMAN

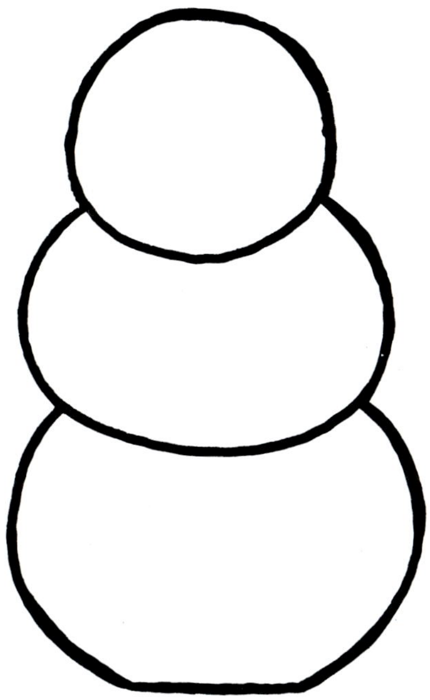

Use carbon paper to trace the snowman pattern on your wood, or make a template to transfer the pattern to the wood. I am using 2" thick basswood. **The grain runs from head to base**. Cut the snowman out using a bandsaw or coping saw.

This photo shows the progression from sawed out blank, roughed out, rounded, and completed carving. The snowman is divided into three sections: the bottom, the middle, and the head. You will need a small v-tool and a drill with a 1/8" bit to complete the project.

Draw a center line completely around the snowman. I have painted my snowman with a blue wash to help the cuts stand out. You don't need to do this to yours.

Draw a center line on the flat sides and then draw the lines to separate the sections.

Draw a circle on the base of the snowman.

Use a coping saw on the line between the bottom and the middle. Saw in the depth of the blade or about 3/8". You are creating a stop between the two sections. Repeat on the three other sides.

Cut back to the saw line on each corner, working your way toward the center line. You make one cut from the direction of the middle to the saw line and then...

make a cut toward the saw line from the direction of the bottom. You are creating a valley between the bottom and the middle. This will take several repetitions of these cuts to remove the wood. Don't try to remove too much wood with each cut. Repeat this process on each corner. I have put on my carving glove but forgot my thumb guard.

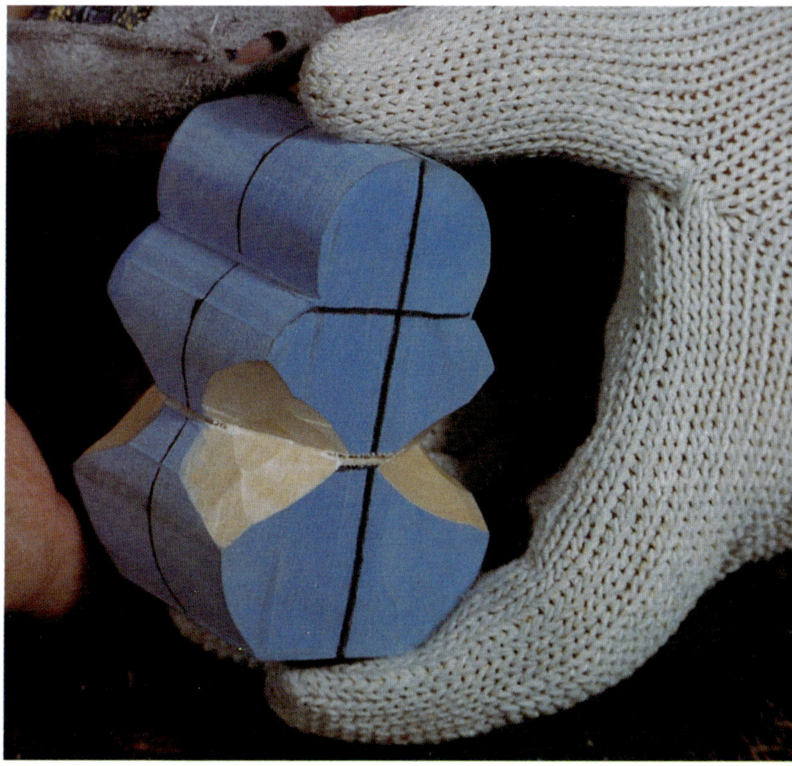

The completed cuts back to the saw line. OK! Now I also have my thumb guard on. I encourage you to wear a carving glove and thumb guard.

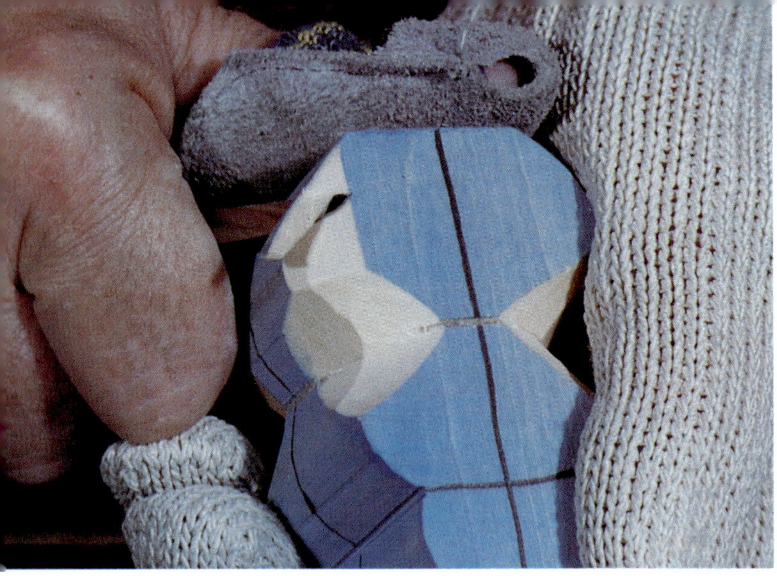

On the bottom section, remove wood from the corner to the center lines.

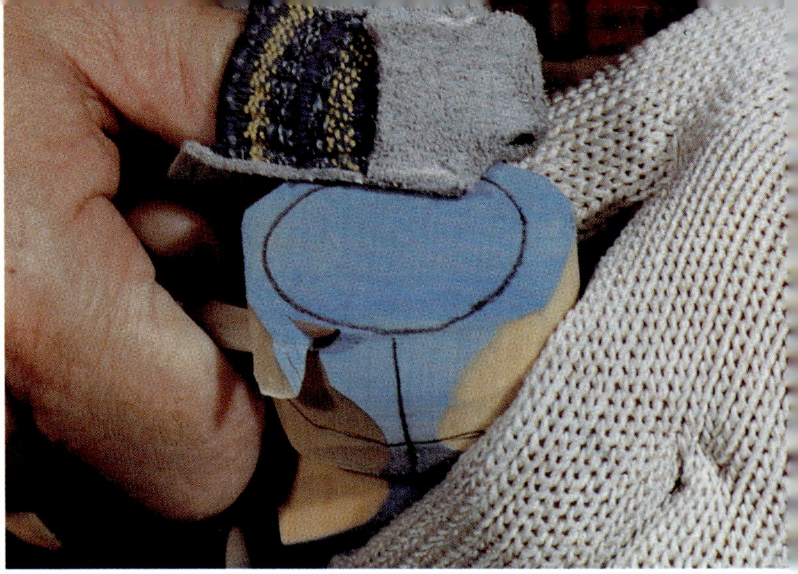

Draw a center line around the bottom section, and then round the bottom from the center line to the circle on the base. You might want to look ahead a couple of pictures to see the center line around the bottom section.

Repeat this process on the three other corners.

The completed work.

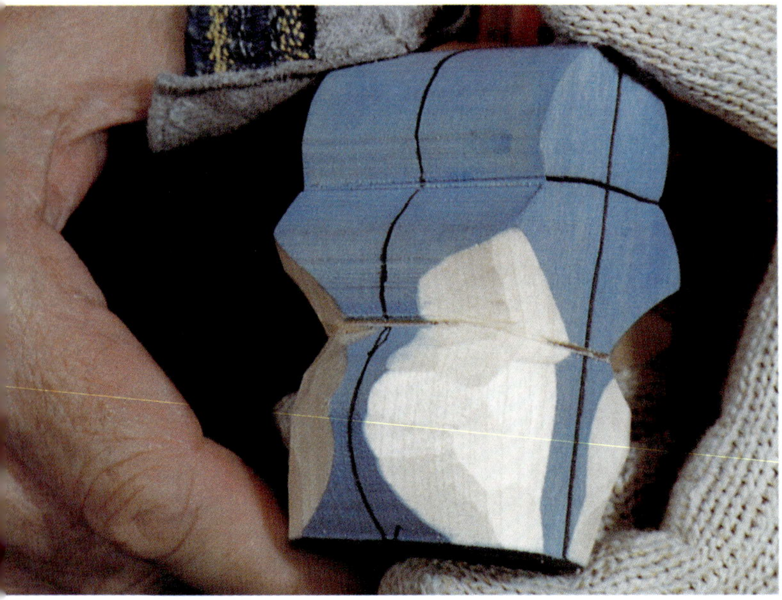

The snowman thus far.

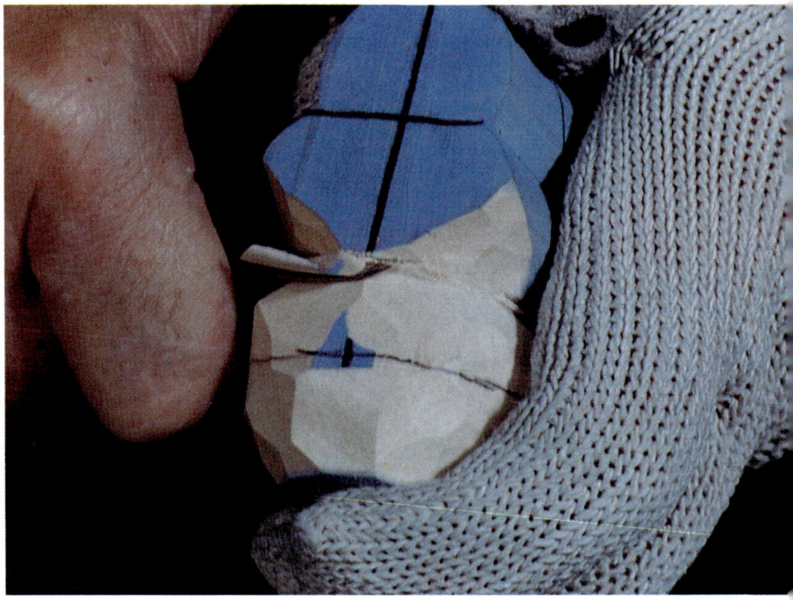

Round the bottom from the center line to the saw line.

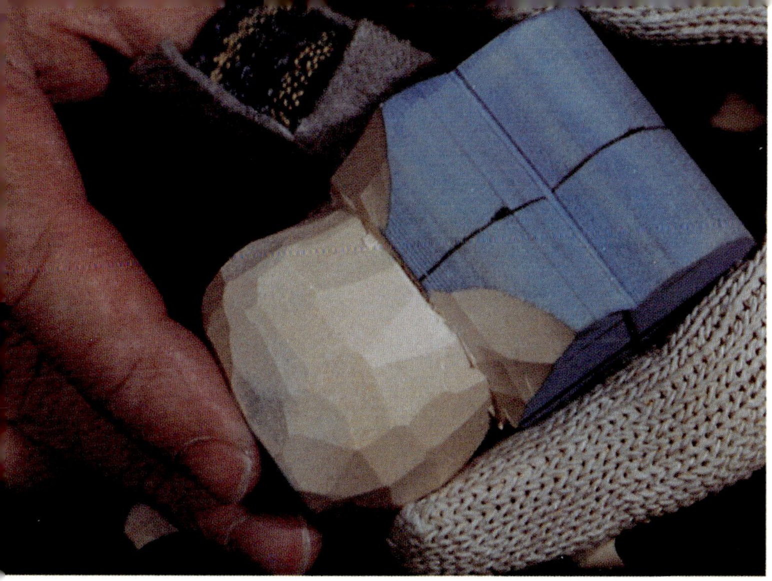

The work so far.

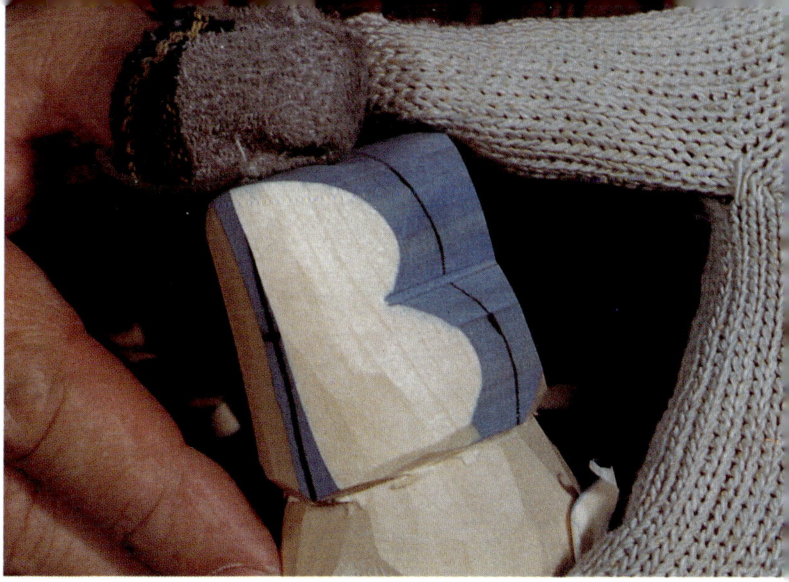

The completed cuts.

On the middle and head, remove wood from the corner to the center lines.

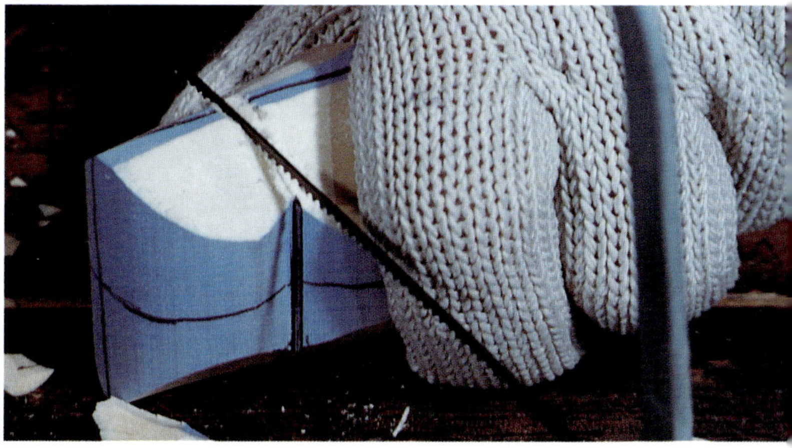

Redraw the line between the middle and the head. Use a coping saw on the line. Saw in the depth of the blade or about 3/8". Repeat on each of the three other sides.

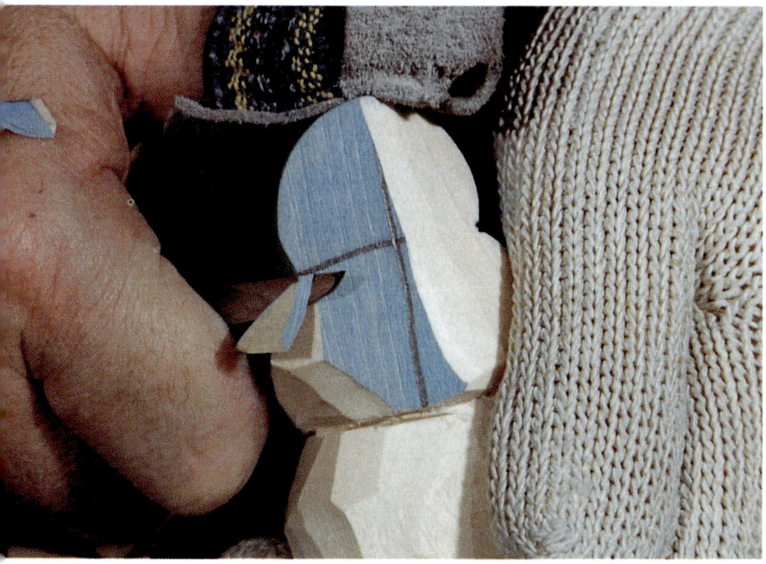

Repeat this process on the three other corners.

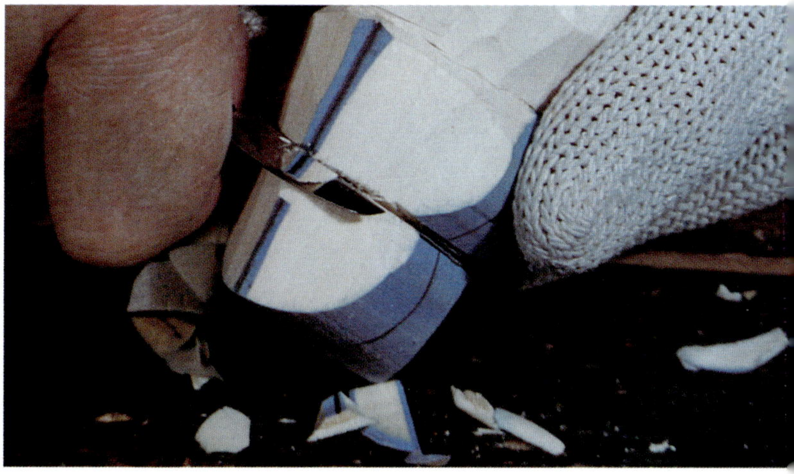

We need to create a valley between the middle and head. Cut back to the saw line. Make one cut from the direction of the head to the saw line and then...

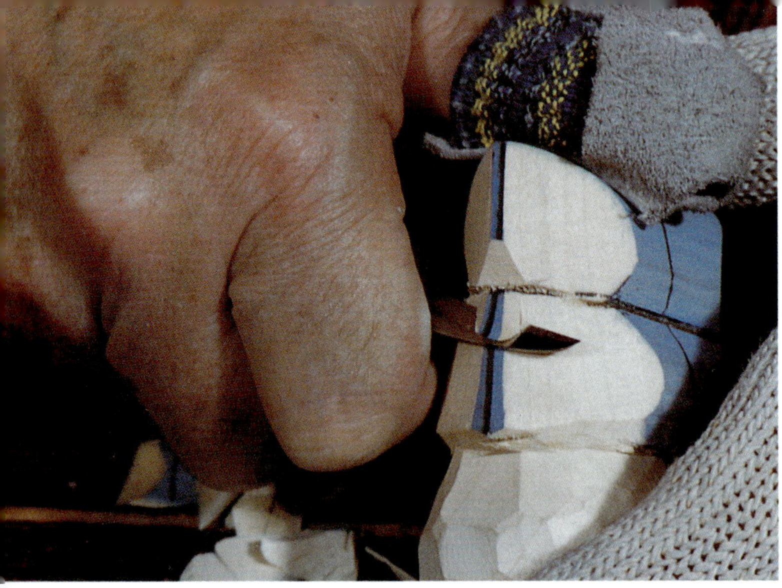

make a cut toward the saw line from the direction of the middle. Work your way completely around the snowman. Remember, don't try to remove too much wood with each cut.

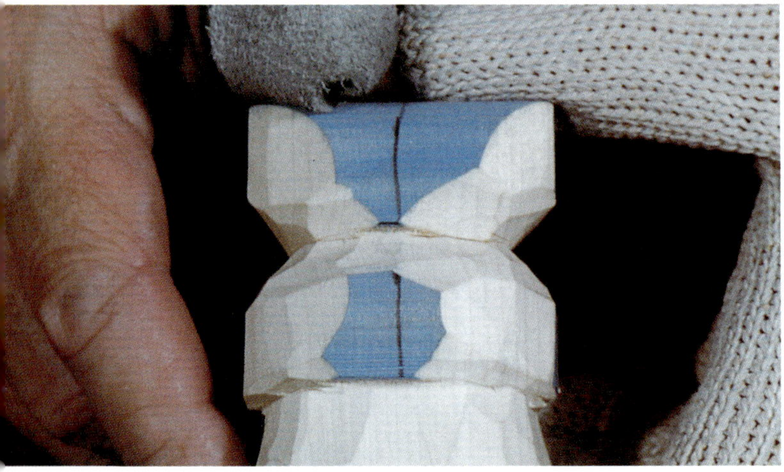

The completed cuts toward the saw line between the middle and the head.

We need to reduce the diameter of the middle section so it is smaller than the bottom section. Remove some wood completely around the middle section. Check your work. If you see that the middle section is still too large, make another trip completely around the snowman removing more wood. Check you work again. Repeat this process until you are happy with the results.

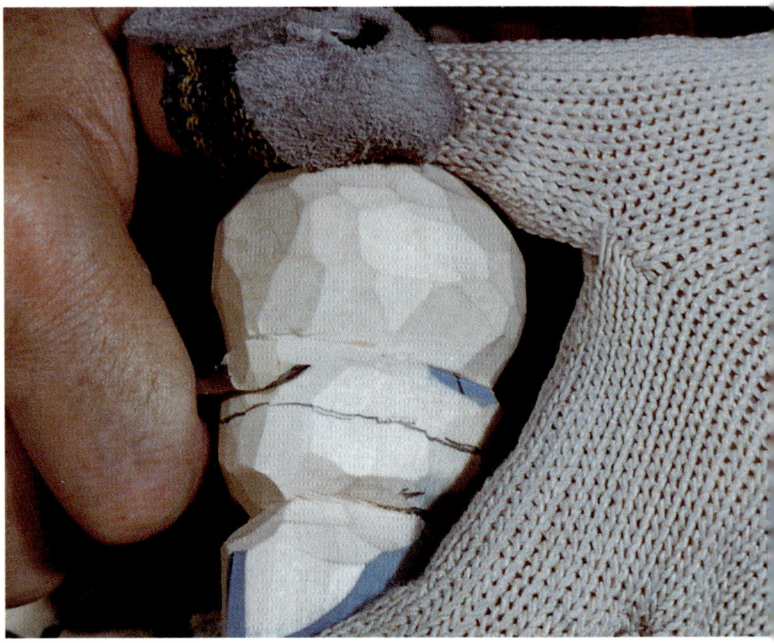

Draw a center line on the middle and round from the center line toward the bottom section and then.....

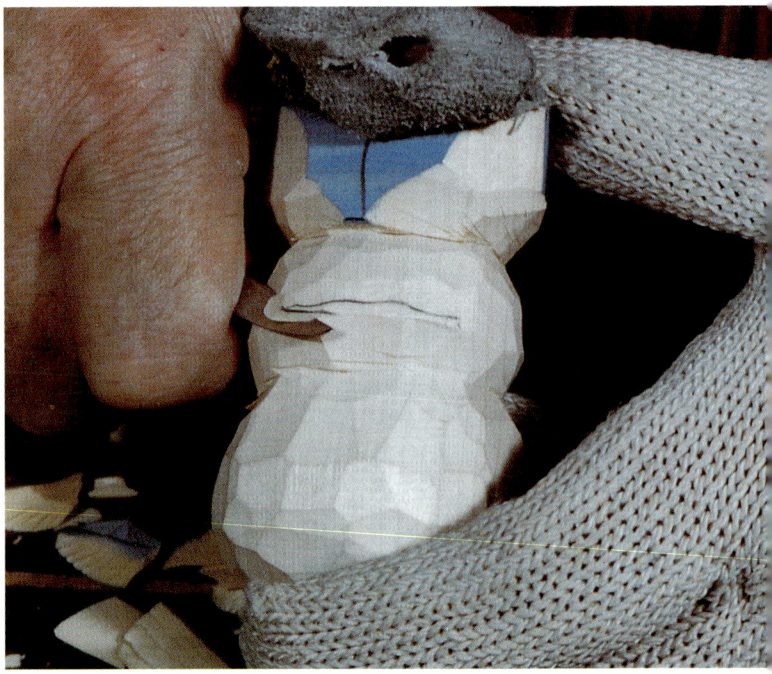

from the center line toward the head.

The completed rounding of the middle section.

Draw a center line around the head and round it from the center line to the top of the head.

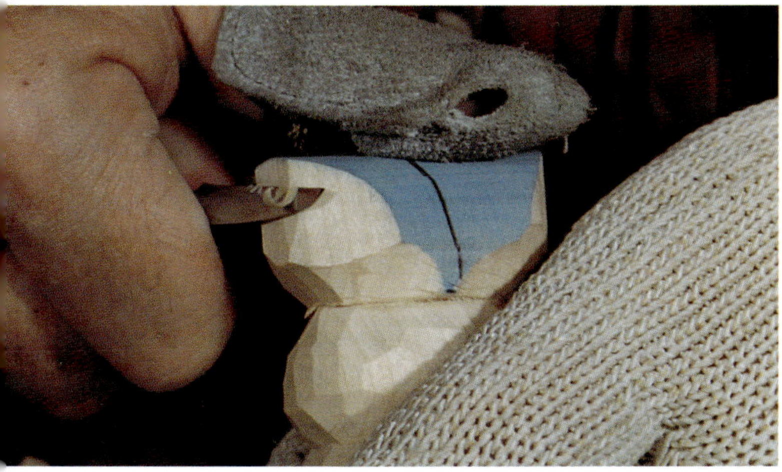

Thin the head.

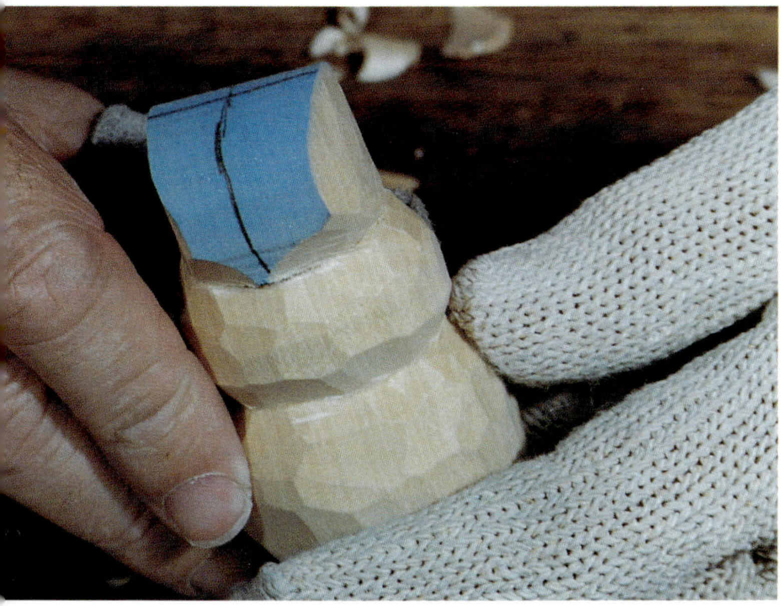

The completed thinning of the head.

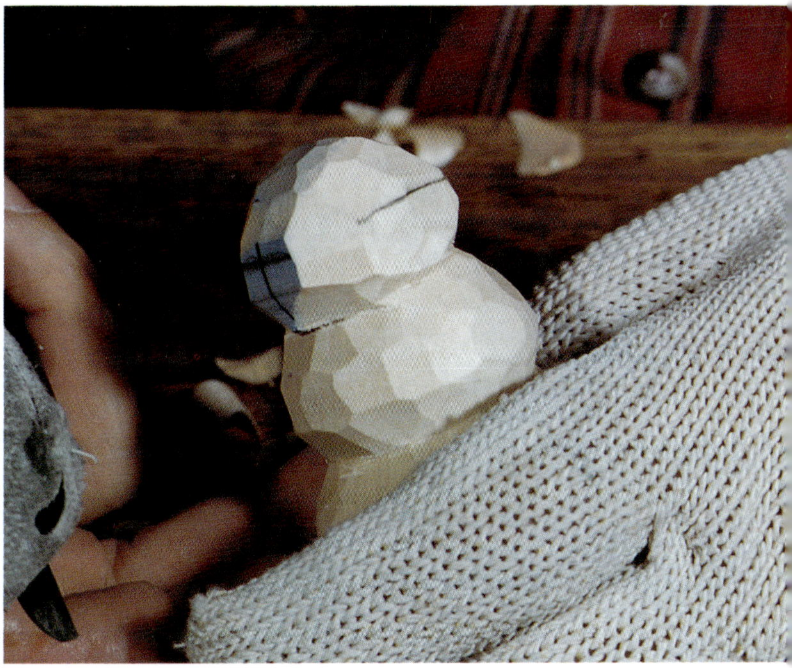

The completed rounding toward the top of the head. Now, round the head from the center line toward the middle section.

Look over the snowman and do any additional rounding that needs to be done. I like to set the carving on a shelf at eye level and look it over. I will usually find some high places, flat places, or a section that needs some rounding.

V-tool the lines of the scarf.

Place three dots for the buttons and then draw on the scarf. Drawing the three buttons will keep you from placing the scarf where the buttons should go.

After the v-tool cuts, use your knife to remove some wood around the scarf. You want to drop the snowman back some from the scarf.

Add some gouge cuts or v-tool cuts to the scarf to add some definition.

I use a 3/16" dowel for the nose. Shape the end of the dowel so it will fit in the hole for the nose. It's best to carve this part of the nose first.

The completed work on the scarf.

Lay out the eyes and nose and then drill a 1/8" hole for the carrot nose.

I think the nose is a little long. This picture illustrates the point that it is much easier to shape the part that goes into the nose hole while the nose is still connected to the dowel.

Cut the nose from the stick. I made the nose a little less than 1/2", including the part that fits in the hole.

The completed nose in the snowman.

Drill a 1/8" hole in each side of the middle section for the twig arms.

Find a branch and cut two arms. I think a "Y" looks good. I make the arms about 1" long. Experimentation and personal preference should rule.

The finished carving of the snowman.

CARVING THE HAT

I carve the top hat from a 1 1/4" square 5" to 6" long basswood board with the grain running the length of the board. The extra length gives some wood for a hand hold. Knock off the corners. Round approximately 2" to 3" of the block.

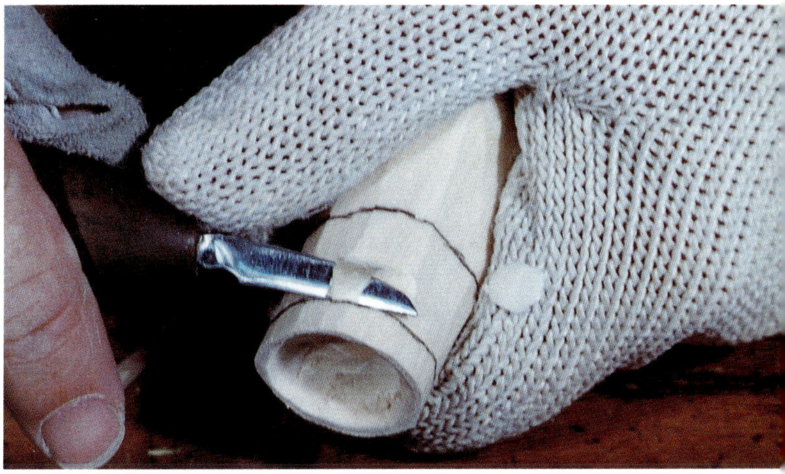

Measure in 1/4" for the brim line and 1" for the top of the hat and draw lines completely around the wood. Incise the 1/4" line and then cut back to the line from the 1" line. The push cut seems to work well for this. **Don't force the knife or you might find a part of the brim laying on the table.** It is easy to cut the brim off the hat.

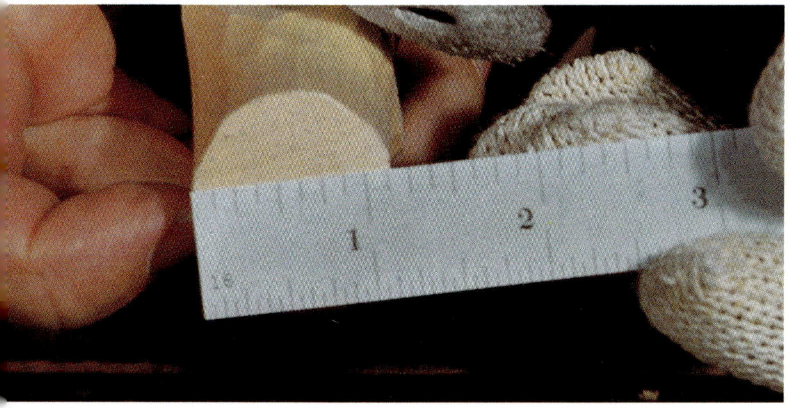

The completed rounding. The brim of the hat should be about 1 1/8" - 1 1/4" in diameter.

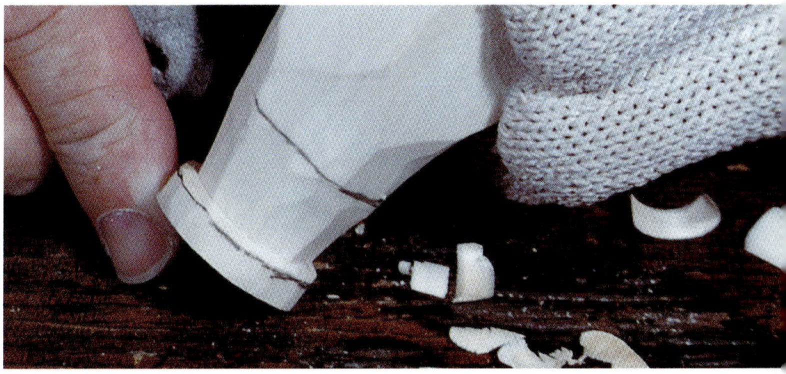

Continue to work around the hat until you have dropped the wood back about 1/4". The hat so far.

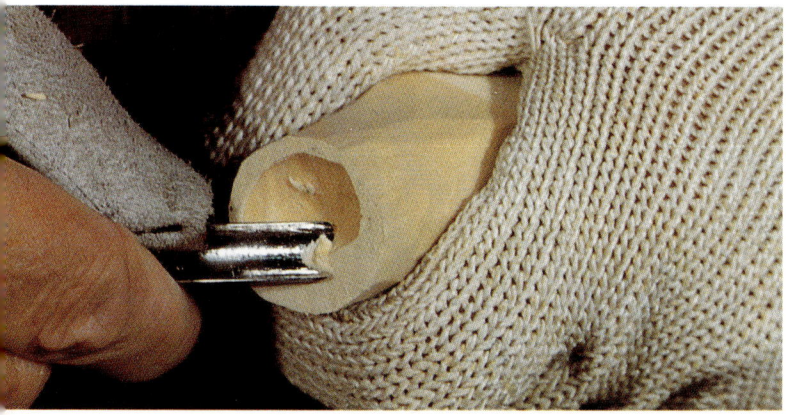

Use a small gouge to clean out some wood on the inside of the hat. This will allow the hat to set on the rounded head of the snowman. If you have a flexible shaft tool and round burr, you can use it for this step.

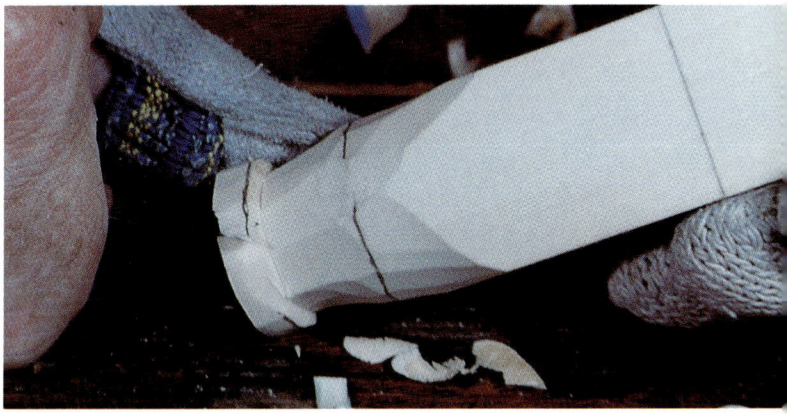

Round the brim of the hat.

I use a small veiner to give the brim a curled up look.

Add some wrinkles with a 3/8" No. 9 or similar gouge and a v-tool. Remember, this is an old hat. Make it look old and worn. Since the hat is small, you want to really think about where the gouge or v-tool might go if it should slip off the wood. **Think before you make a cut!**

Use a small v-tool to add a band round the hat.

I use a black acrylic wash to paint the hat. The completed hat.

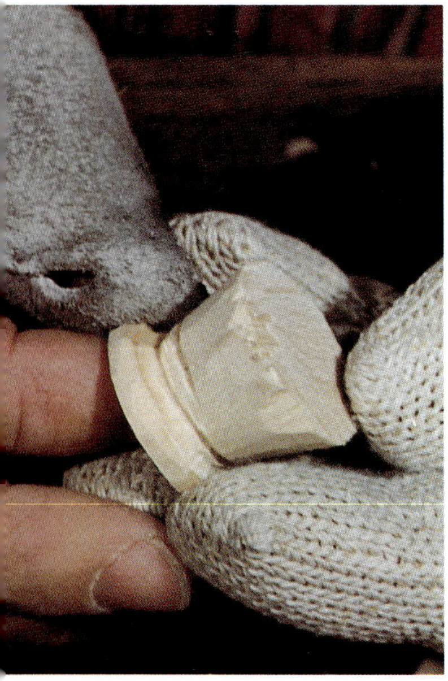

Saw the hat on the 1" line to separate it from the work stick.

Round the top edge of the hat.

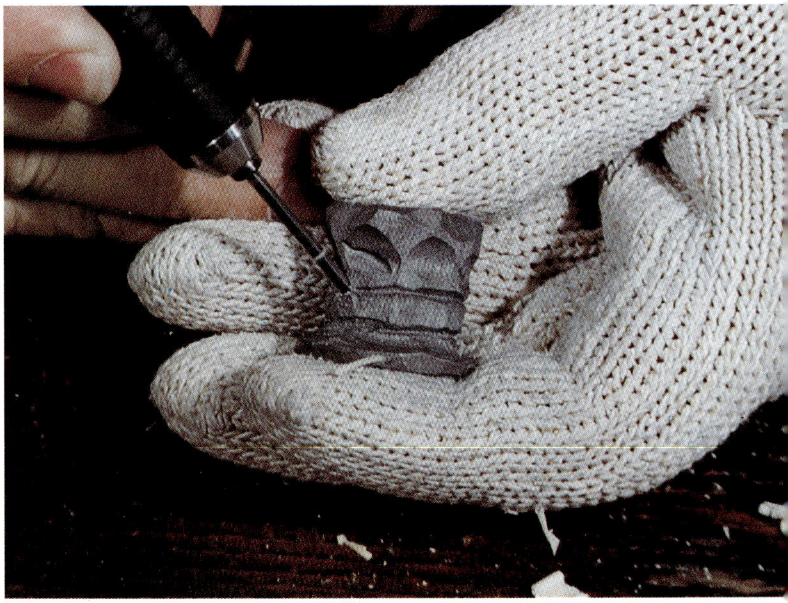

If you plan to add a toothpick flower, you need to drill a small hole slightly above the band of the hat. You want the flower to appear to be held by the band.

CARVING THE FLOWER

We can dress the top hat up a bit by adding a colorful flower. OK! I know this is a snowman and flowers don't normally bloom in the winter. So..... it's an artificial flower. The snowman is not going to know the difference! I carve the flower from a toothpick. When carving a tooth pick, don't use a lot of pressure or you'll break the toothpick before you have the flower carved. Draw two lines around the tooth pick. Measure in approximately 1/2" for one line and 3/4" for the other. An X-acto™ knife with a #11 blade works well.

Rotate the toothpick and make the next cut toward the 1/2" line. One of the keys to carving a flower is to start each knife cut on the 3/4" line and end it at the 1/2" line your first time around the toothpick.

Place your knife on the 3/4" line and make a very thin shaving cut toward the 1/2" line. You don't want to dig the knife into the wood. When your knife reaches the 1/2" line, gently roll your knife and the flower petal perpendicular to the shaft of the toothpick. This will help the petal lay away from the shaft.

After the first trip around the toothpick, continue to rotate the toothpick making cuts around the diameter of the toothpick until you have finished the flower or it breaks loose. The thinner the cuts, the more times you will be able to "go around" the shaft making petals; the more petals, the fuller the flower.

The completed flower. Don't become discouraged; it usually takes me about ten flowers before I get one I like. I think the work is worth it. The flower adds a lot to the hat.

I paint the flower with acrylics straight from the bottle. A green stem and yellow flower. Of course, you can use whatever color you like for the flower.

The flower is glued into the hat. I use tweezers to position it.

FINISHING THE SNOWMAN

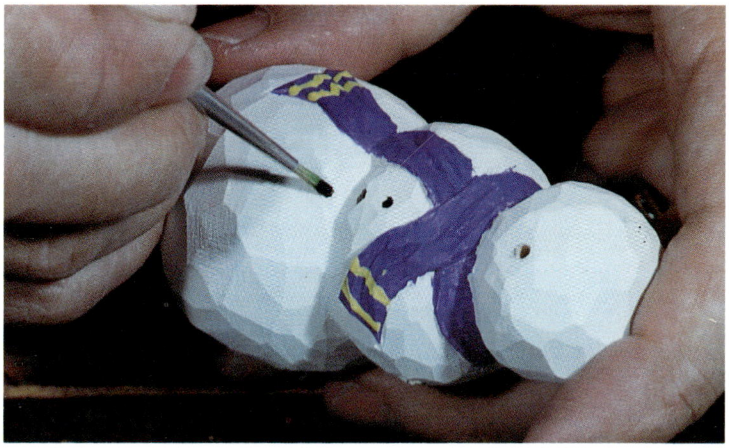

I paint the snowman with acrylic paints straight from the bottle. I give the snowman several coats of white. When it's dry, I paint the scarf and then add black buttons, eyes, and mouth.

I paint a 1/4" oak base with white paint. I let some of the wood show.

I glue in the carrot nose and then paint it. I find this works better for me.

After the snowman is attached to the base with a screw, I use DecoArt™ Snow-Tex™ to add a snow look texture to the base. You can completely paint the snowman with Snow-Tex™. There is a snowman in the gallery that has been painted with Snow-Tex™. I really think it looks nice but tends to cover up the knife marks. It's your snowman, finish it the way you like.

Glue in the twig arms and glue on the hat.

The completed snowman.

SLEEPING SANTA

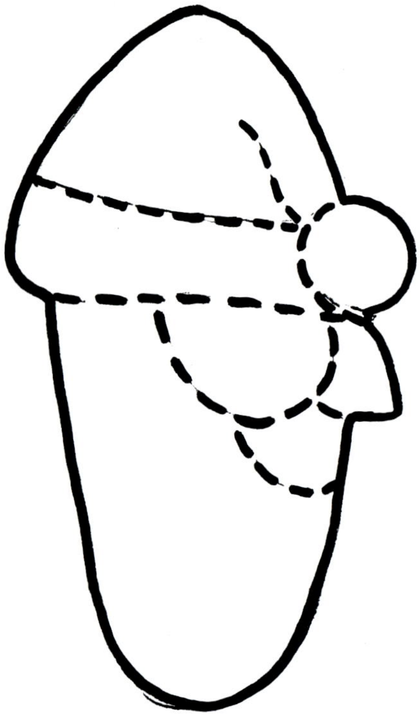

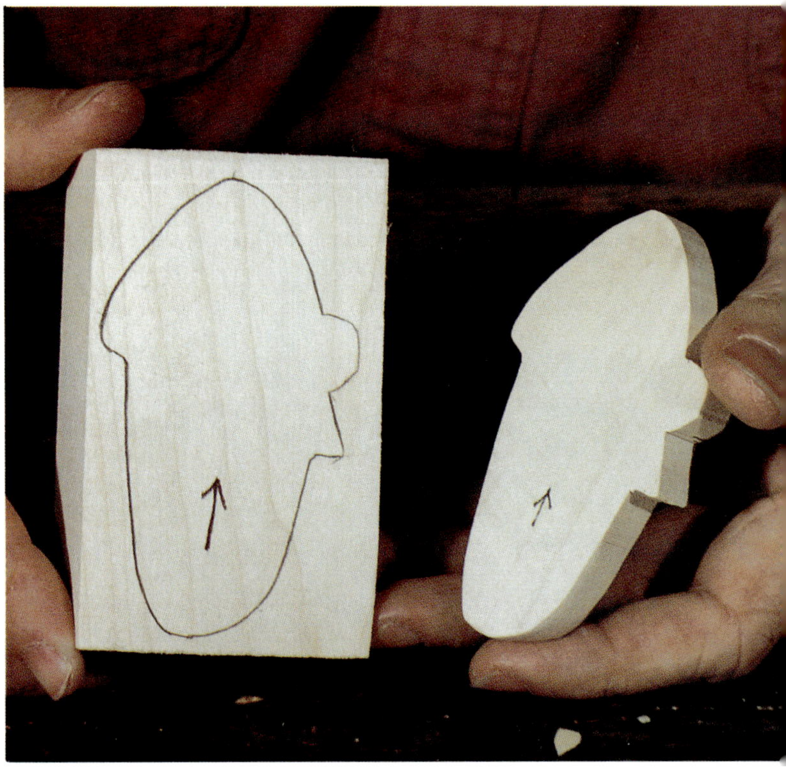

Use carbon paper to trace the Santa pattern on your wood. I am using 1 3/8" thick basswood. **The grain runs from top to bottom**. Cut the Santa out using a bandsaw or coping saw. At the right is a template I use over and over. It eliminates having to use carbon paper each time I want to transfer the pattern to my wood. You will need a small v-tool and a small veiner to complete the Santa. If you only have a knife, you still can do the project but will have to leave off some details. Those details would include the hair on the beard and the texturing of the fur on the hat.

If you vary the thickness of the wood, you will get a different look for your Santa. The one on the left is 1 1/4" thick, the one in the middle is 1 3/8" thick, and the one on the right is 1 1/2" thick. You could do a really thin Santa out of 1" thick wood. Experiment with pattern reduction or enlargement to create different sizes.

Draw a center line completely around the Santa. Split the distance between the center line and add another line for the ball of the hat. I am wearing a carving glove and thumb guard. I encourage you to do so as well.

Cut back to the stop cut. I am using the pull cut.

Make a stop cut on the ball line.

Continue to remove wood the complete width of the Santa. You will be causing the ball to stand out from the hat.

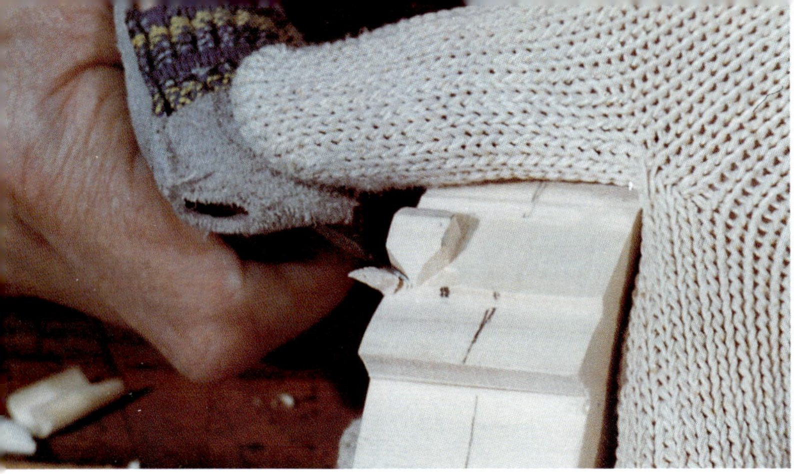

Remove the wood from each corner of the ball. I am using a push cut to complete this task.

Repeat the rounding process on the other side. Start rounding just above the ball and remove wood toward the center line.

The Santa thus far. Draw two lines to make the nose. The nose should be a little wider than you think it should be. It's easier to remove wood later but impossible to add wood you have removed in the rounding out process.

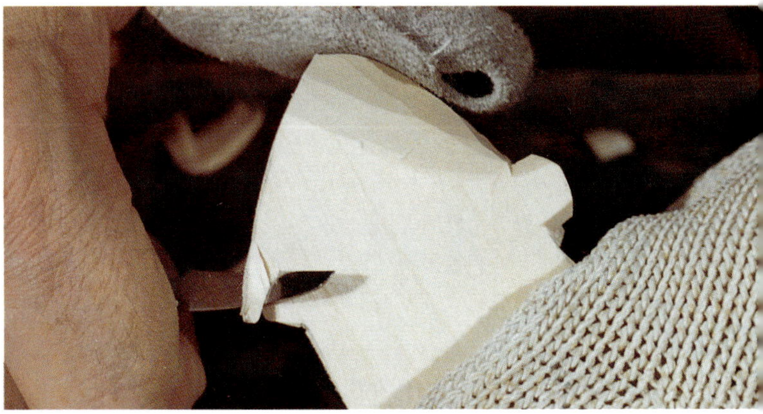

Begin the rounding process on the back of the hat.

We are now ready to round the hat. Remove some wood from the edge, rounding the hat toward the center line. Don't cut into the nose line. You can see that I started rounding just at the base of the nose.

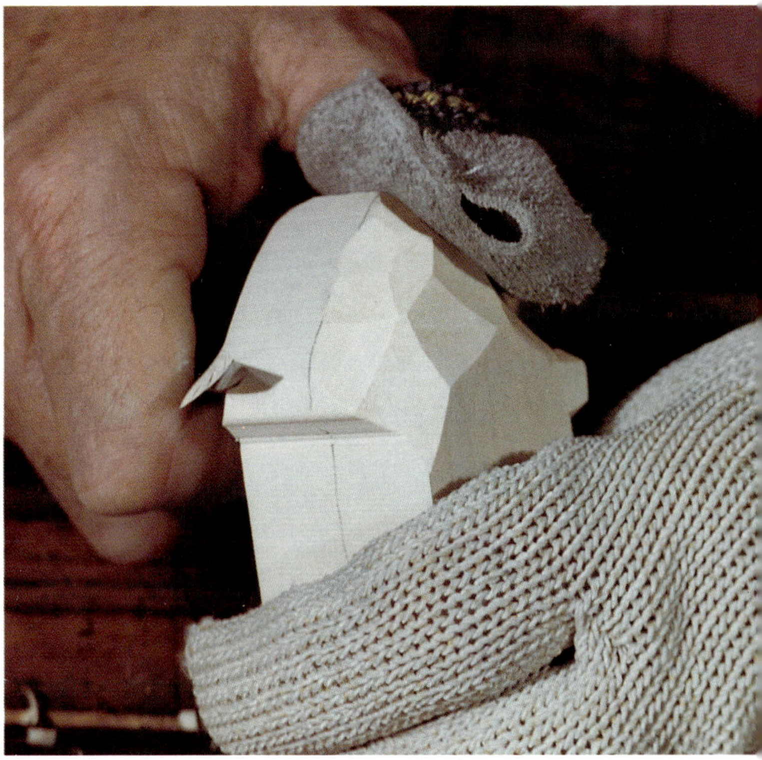

This photo shows the work completed from the previous step. Complete the process on the other side of the back of the hat.

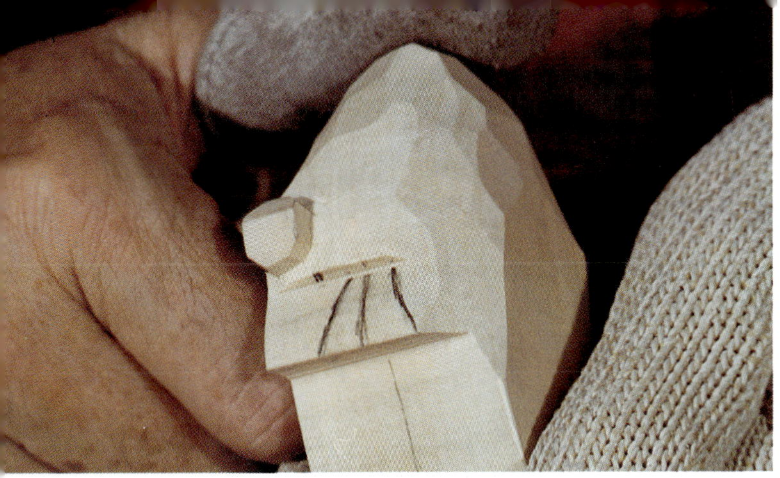

The completed rounding of the hat.

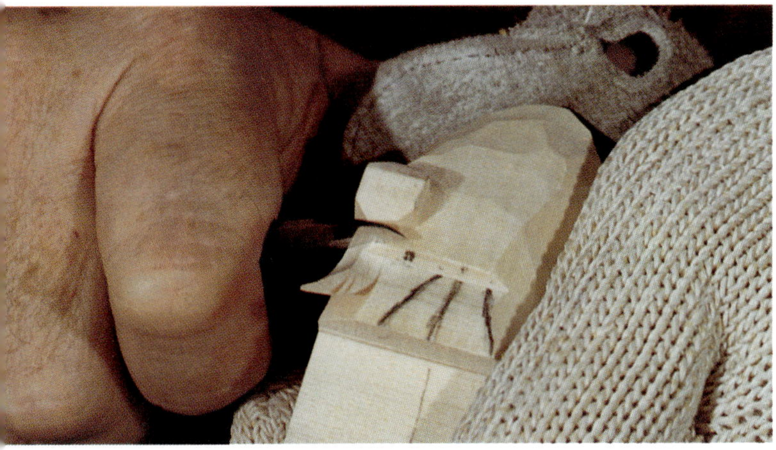

Make a stop cut under the ball and then cut back to the stop, removing the wood from the cheek. Don't cut into the nose line. This will take a combination of several stop cuts and removing wood back to the stop. Take your time. Don't try to remove too much wood with each cut.

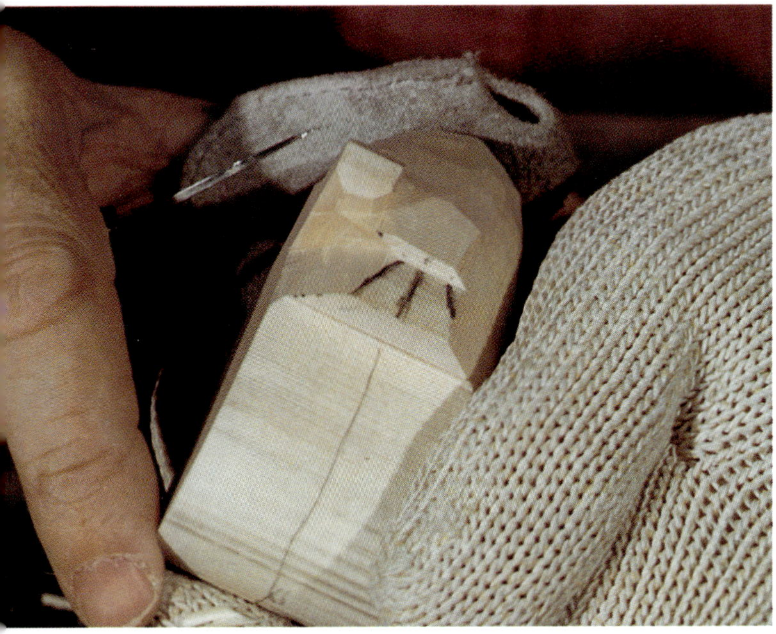

The completed wood removal from under the ball and from the cheek.

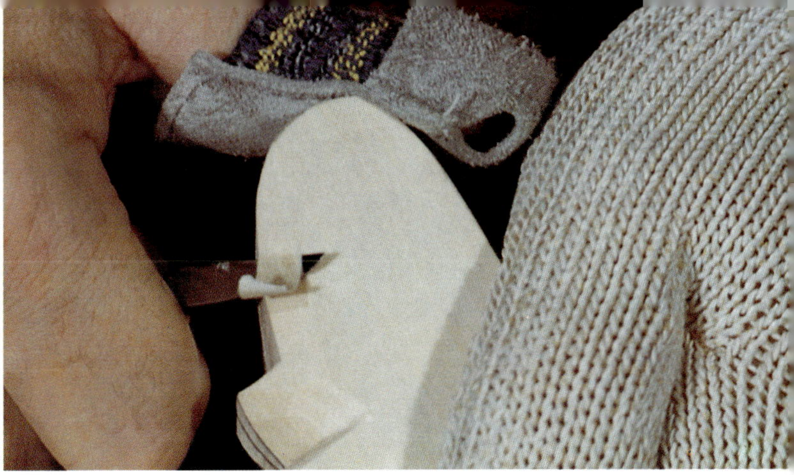

Starting at the base of the nose, round the beard toward the center line. Work you way around to the back of the Santa, rounding as you go.

The completed rounding on the beard and back.

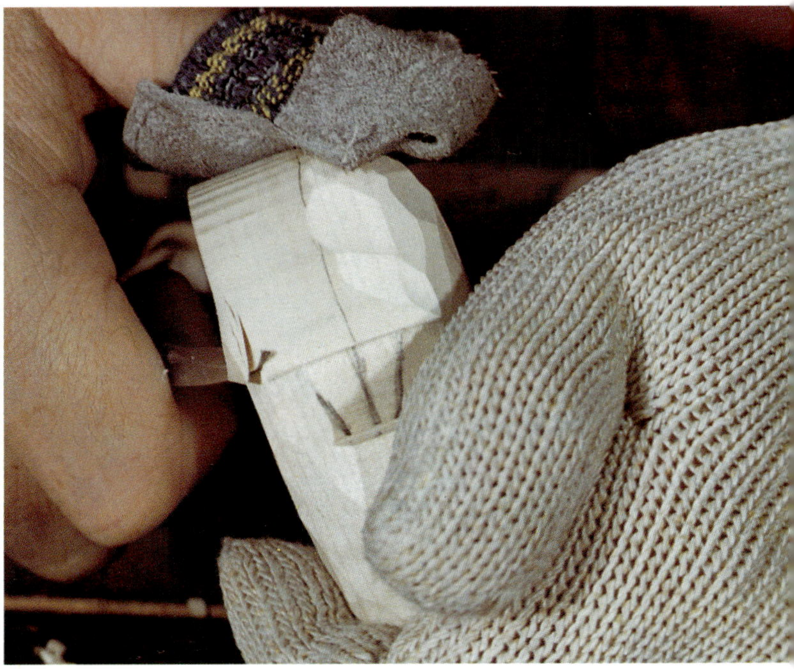

Round the other side. Work the beard and hair into the center line.

This photo shows the completed rounding of the hat, beard, and hair. Draw a line for the edge of the hat completely around the Santa.

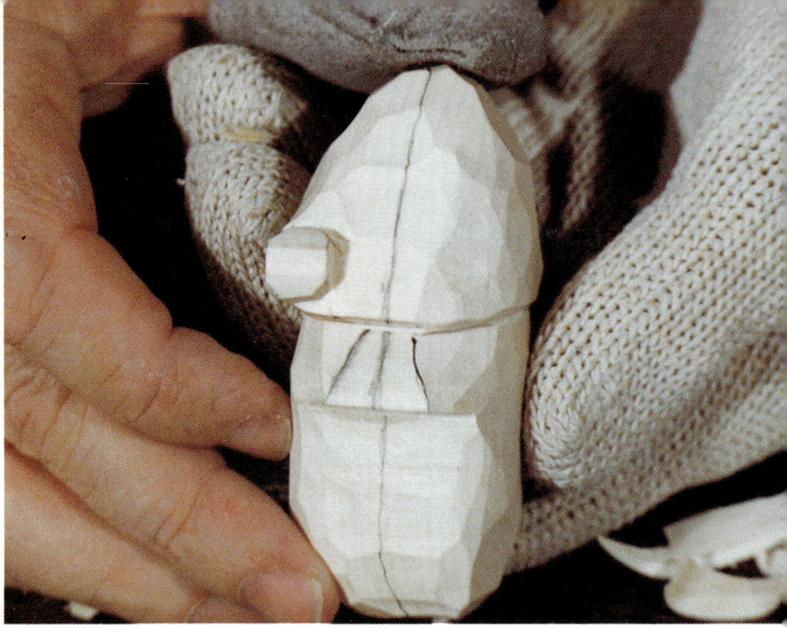

The completed work of separating the hat from the cheeks and hair.

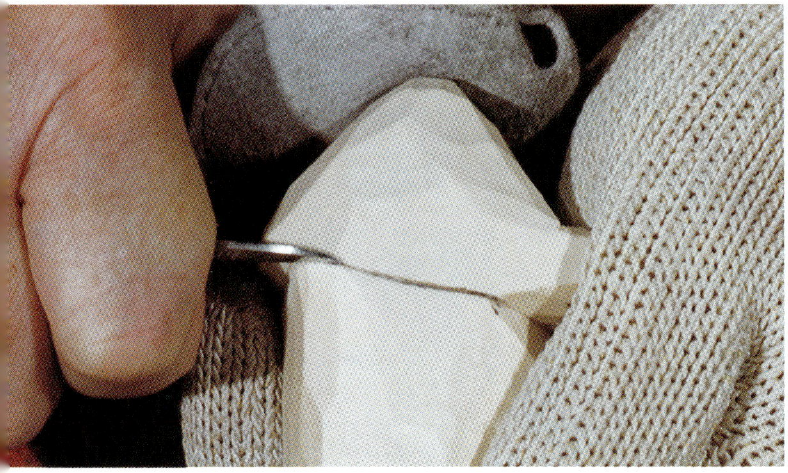

Make a stop cut on the line completely around the Santa.

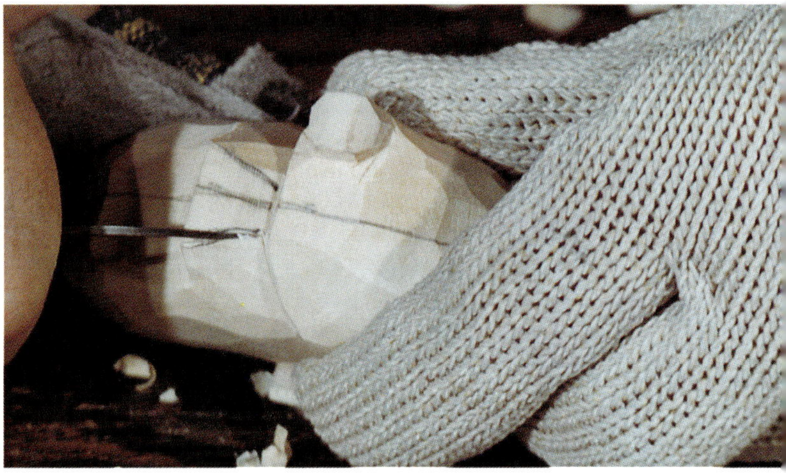

Make a stop cut straight in on the nose line. This is the first step in removing the wood from the side of the nose.

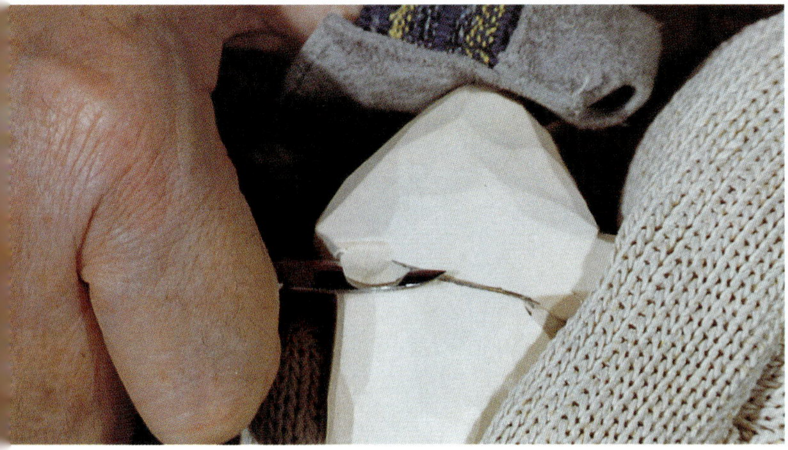

Cut back to the stop cut. This action will separate the hat from the cheeks and the hair. I drop the cheek area and hair back about 1/8". The depth you drop the wood back will determine how much the hat stands out from the cheeks and hair. Work completely around the hat.

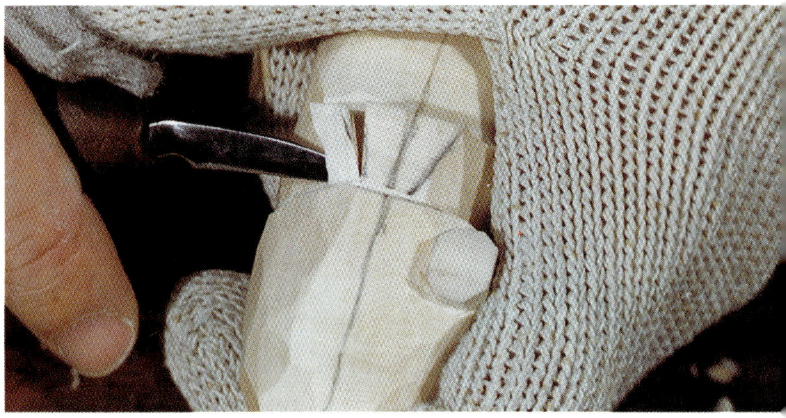

Cut back to the edge of the hat from the bottom of the nose. Make sure your knife point does not stick into the side of the nose. I am using the push cut. After making the cut, make a stop cut at the edge of the hat to remove the wood. It may take a combination of push cuts and stop cuts to remove the wood.

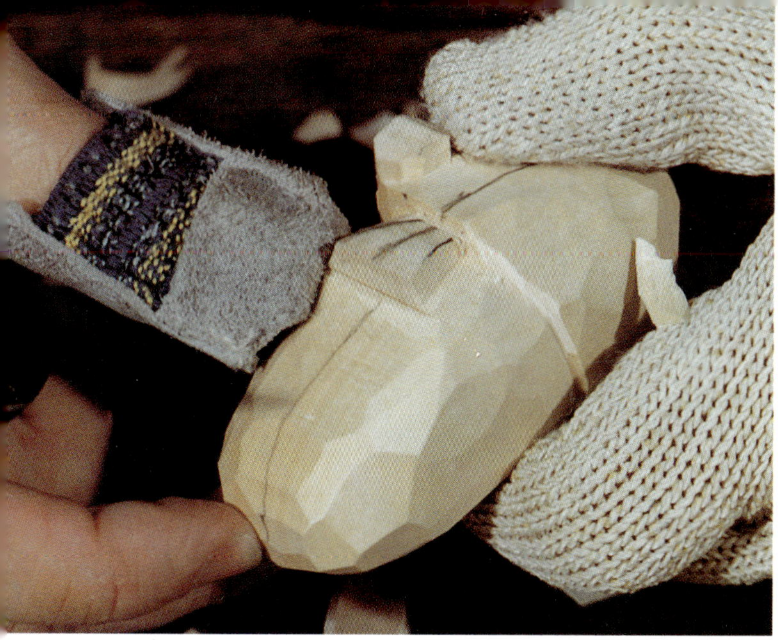

The removal of wood from one side of the nose. You can see how the nose stands out from the cheek.

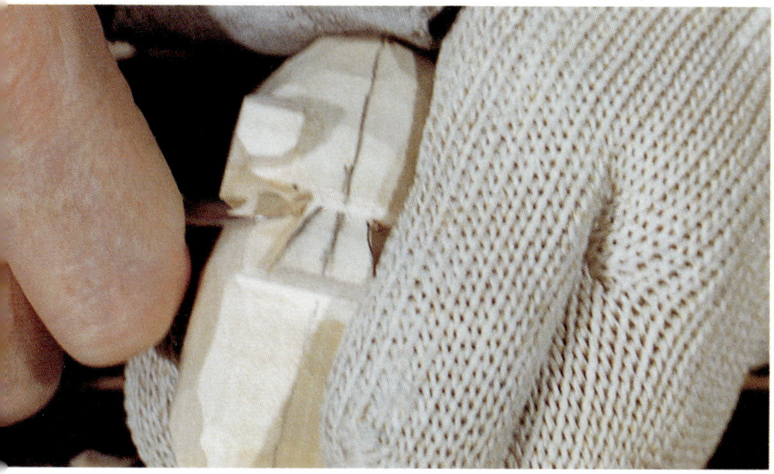

Repeat the process on the other side of the nose.

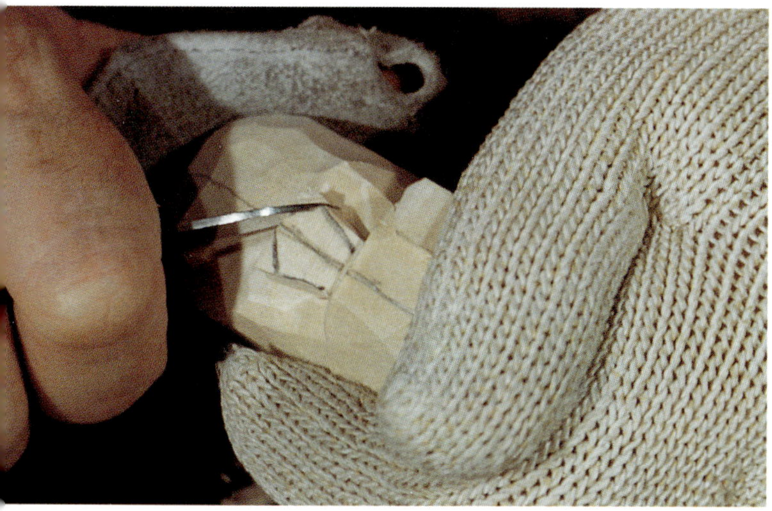

Draw a line on each corner of the nose and cut the wood away. This begins the rounding process on the nose.

Round the nose.

The nose has been rounded. The Santa thus far.

Draw on the cheeks. I use a set of dividers to help me lay out the cheek lines. I place one divider on the center line of the nose and the other at the center of the side of the head. Using the dividers helps me make sure that the cheek lines are even on both sides. Repeat the process on the other side. A compass will work just as well.

Draw on the cheek lines. I use a line perpendicular to the center line to determine the bottom of the cheeks.

Cut back to the stop cuts and pop out the wedge. The last two stop cuts and the removal of the wood have defined the cheek line, moustache, and bottom of the nose.

Make a stop cut on the cheek line where it touches the nose. Repeat the other side.

Cut a stop along the complete length of the cheek line.

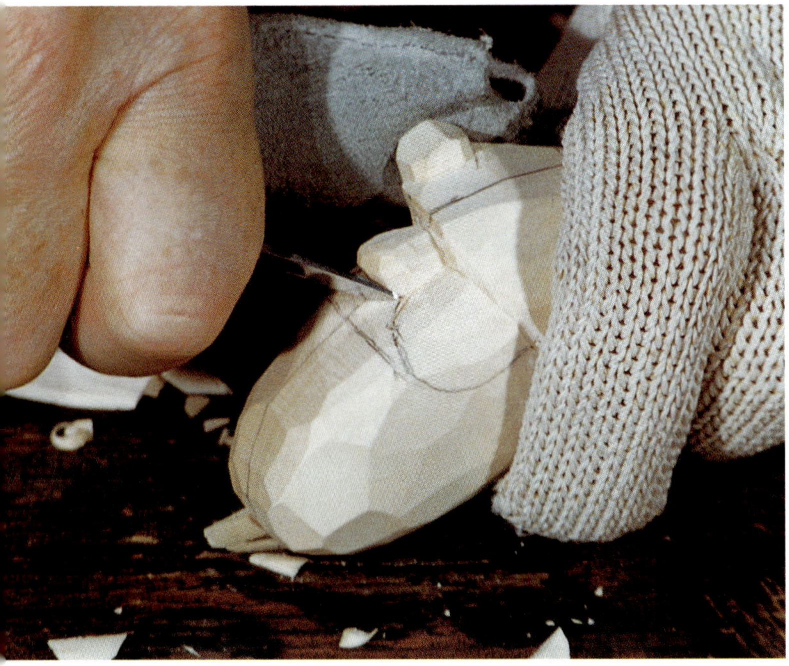

Make a stop cut at the corner of the nose. Repeat the other side.

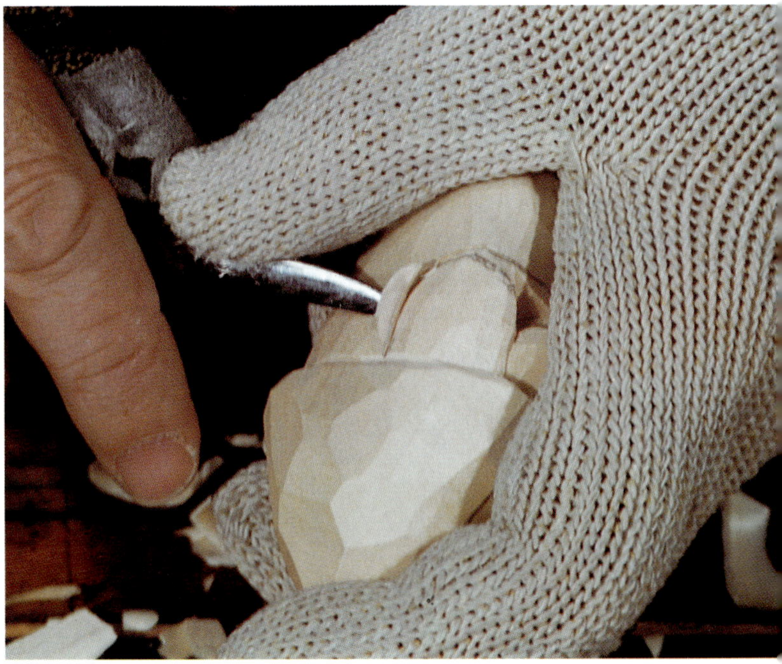

Cut back to the stop, removing wood along the line.

This photo shows the completed removal of wood around one cheek.

Repeat the process on the left side of the Santa.

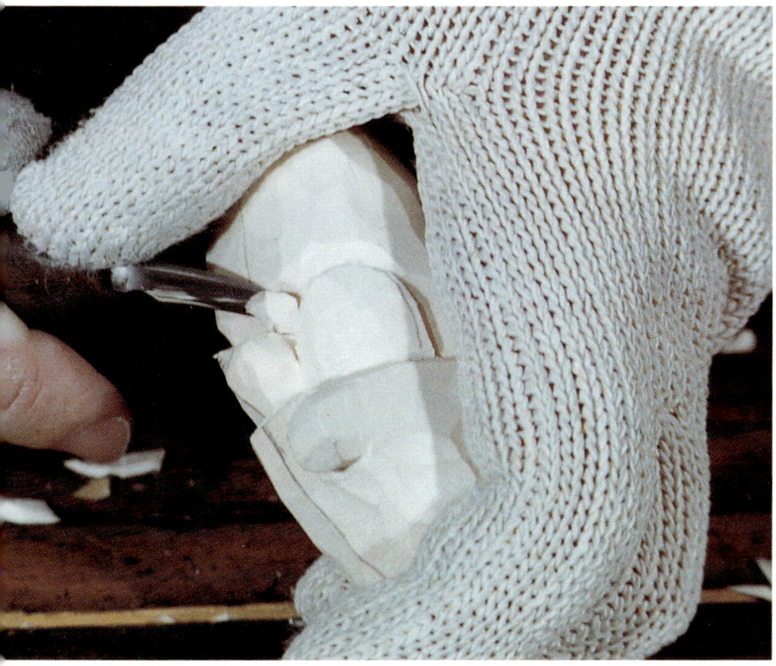

I am finishing the removal of the wood around the cheek.

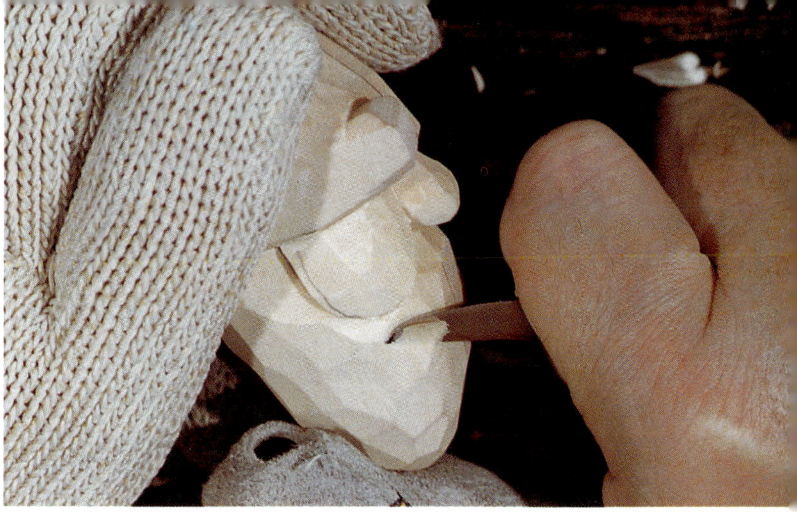

Drop the moustache area back some below the cheek. This will help the cheek to stand out. Repeat on the other side.

Draw the moustache and cut a stop on each side of the V at the center line of the moustache.

Cut back to the stop cuts, popping out the wood to form the inside of the mouth.

If you have a small v-tool, run it from the inside of the mouth along the moustache line. If you don't have a v-tool, you need to make a stop cut on the moustache line and cut back to it to remove some wood. Repeat on the other side.

Round the cheeks into the moustache. You want to knock off any sharp edges.

The completed removal of wood below the moustache.

Draw a line for the edge of the ball. Make a stop cut on the line and cut back to it from the direction of the hat and then from the ball. You are creating a valley. The next photo shows the completed work.

Taper the moustache back toward the cheek.

Round the ball.

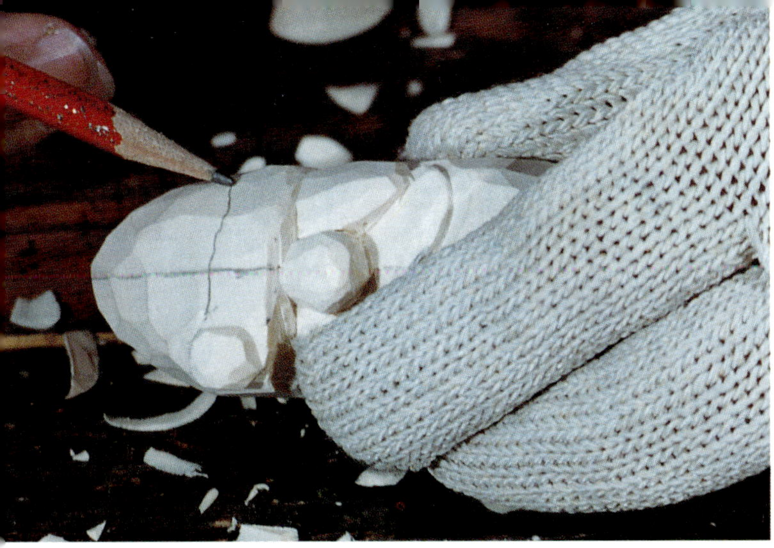

Draw the fur line completely around the hat.

The Santa thus far.

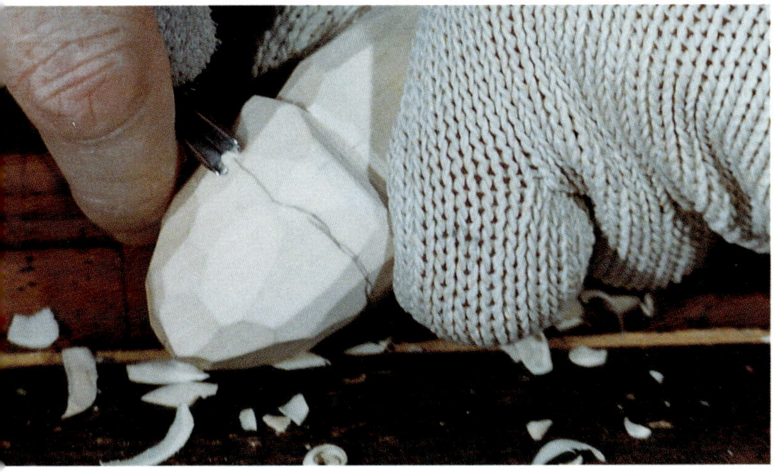

V-tool the line. If you don't have a v-tool, you will have to use the stop cut approach.

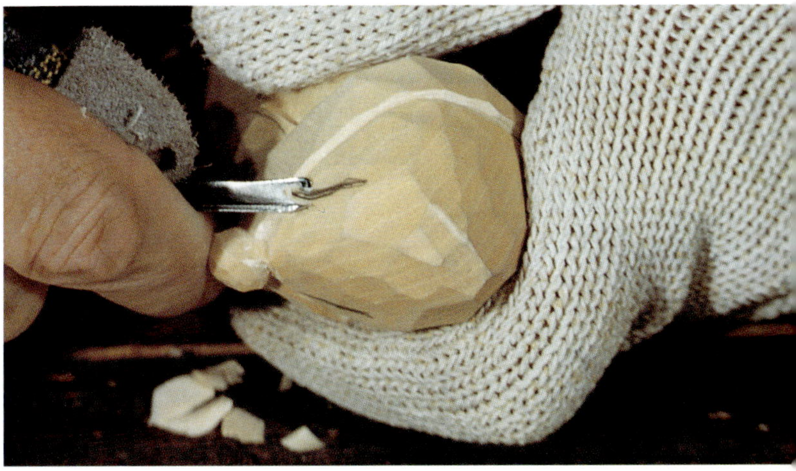

Add a v-tool cut on each side of the ball toward the middle of the hat to create the fold of the hat.

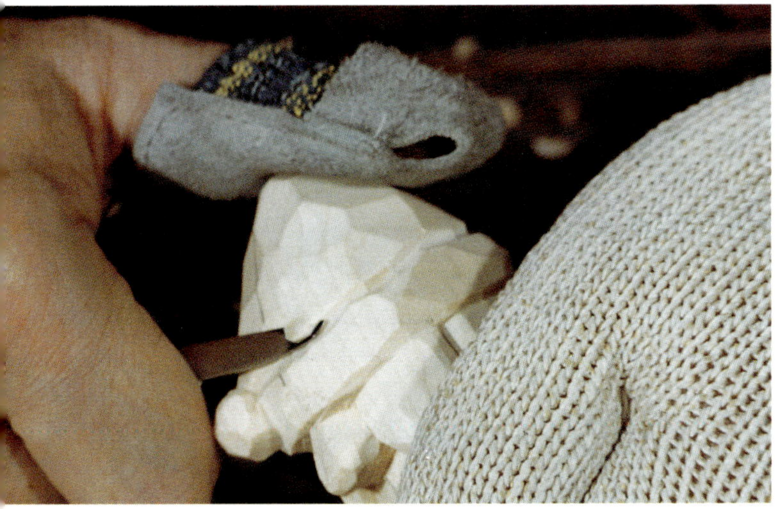

After using the v-tool, drop the hat back from the fur. This will help the fur stand out from the rest of the hat.

Use a 3/8" No. 9 gouge or similar to add some large wrinkles to the hat. If you don't have a gouge, you will need to skip this step.

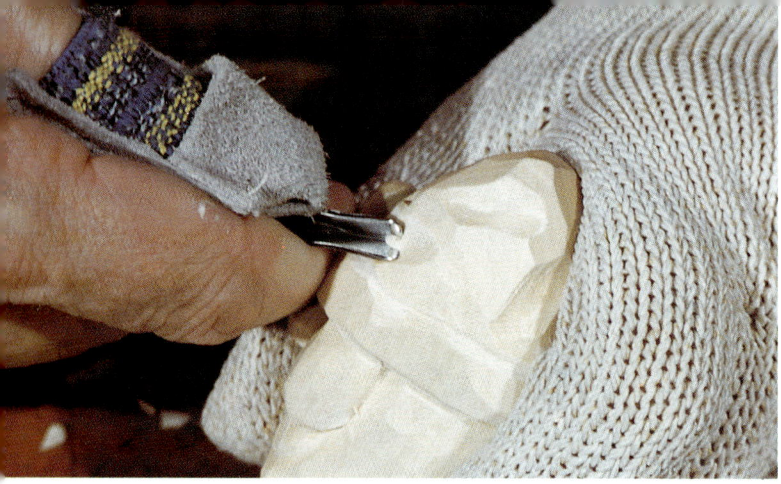

V-tool inside the gouge marks to make the wrinkles more defined.

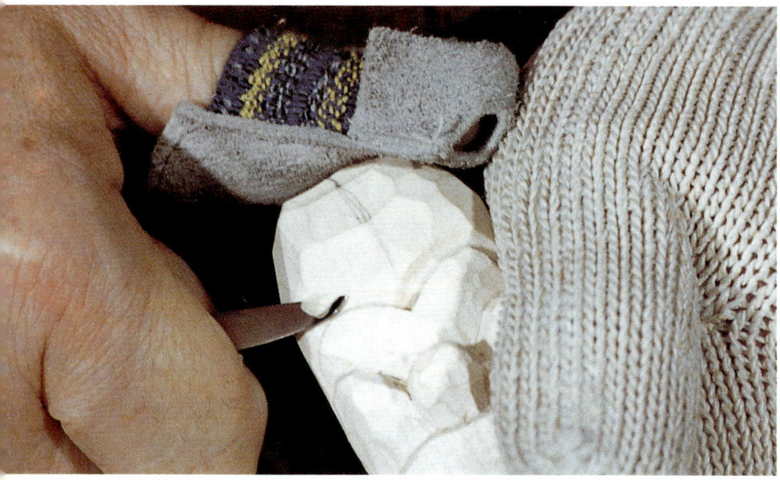

Drop the beard back some from the moustache. This will help the moustache stand out.

Draw a line for the lower lip and use a small veiner just under the line to form the lip. You can complete this step with your knife. You can make stop cuts along the lip line and cut back to them from the beard.

Once you have created the lower lip you need to use your knife to trim some wood out of the inside of the mouth. This will help the mouth have an open look. Don't trim away any wood that forms the lip or moustache.

Use a small v-tool to add detail to the beard and hair. If you don't have a v-tool, you will have to skip this detailing. Your Santa will just have smooth hair and beard.

Continue to use the v-tool completely around the beard and hair.

The completed v-tool work on the beard and hair.

Run a small v-tool through the veiner cuts to add even more definition.

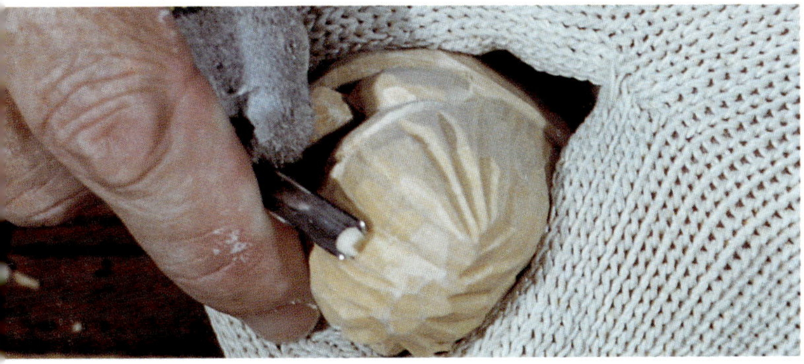

Use a veiner to go over the high points on the beard and hair. These cuts will create small valleys between the v-tool cuts.

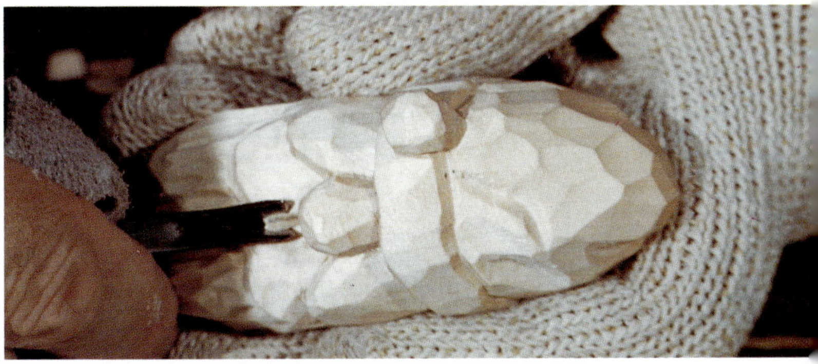

Use the v-tool to make a division in the moustache.

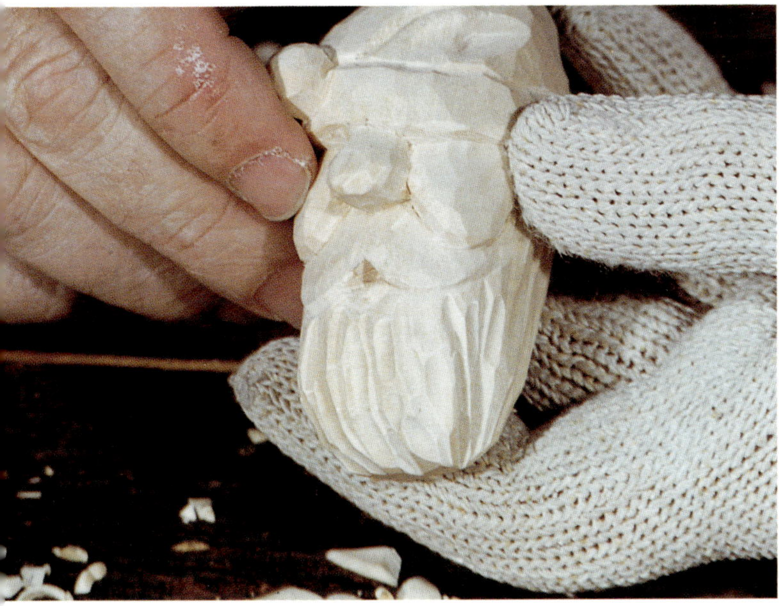

You can see how the veiner has added some definition to the beard. Look back to the picture that showed the completed v-tool work for a comparison.

Draw some hair lines on the moustache and v-tool them. You can also use the veiner between the v-tool lines to add more definition.

Use a small veiner to add definition to the fur on the cap. Work your way completely around the hat. Don't forget to add some definition to the ball.

The completed carving of the Santa. At this point, I like to look over the Santa and use my knife to remove any burrs, chips, or saw marks.

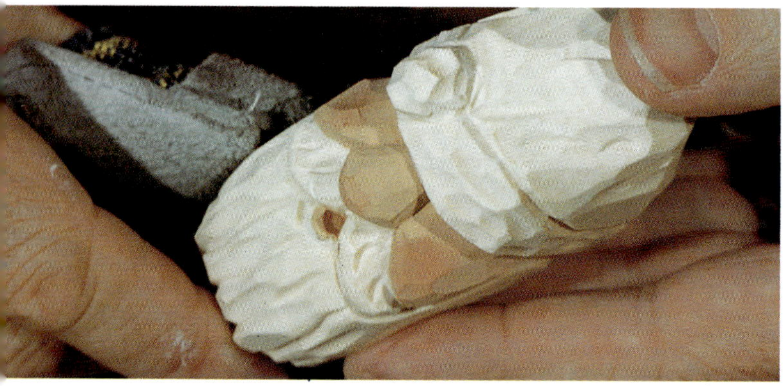

I paint the Santa with acrylics starting with the flesh color. I add some blush to the cheeks.

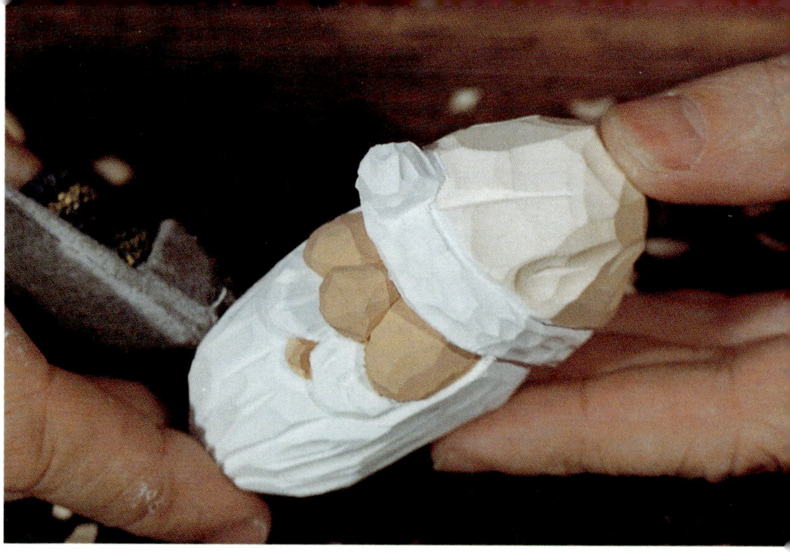

After the flesh is dry, I add the white. I left the cheek blush off this one so you could see the difference. I think the blush really adds to the carving.

Finally, I add the red. Once the red is dry, I spray the carving with a coat of sealer.

I have added the screw eye to the top of the Santa.

GALLERY

JEFF

JEFF